For my amazing little girls, Éva Loren and Isla-Mai, and my awesome husband, Jamie, for always believing I could do this. And to every Mum who has ever doubted themselves – this is for you

Me, Jamie and our awesome tiny humans

KEEP IN TOUCH

One of the best parts about writing my blog has been hearing from other mums and sharing our tales of motherhood. I would love to hear from you.

Share and tag your photos of *BONKERS: A Real Mum's Hilariously Honest Tales of Motherhood, Mayhem & Mental Health* using the #BONKERS hashtag

Visit **The Baby Bible** Blog
www.the-baby-bible.com
Facebook.com/theoliviasiegl
Instagram.com/oliviasiegl
Twitter.com/oliviasiegl
Join the secret Facebook Group hello@everymummovement.com

Join **The Every Mum Movement**
www.everymummovement.com
Facebook.com/everymummovement
Instagram.com/everymummovement
Twitter.com/theeverymum

CONTENTS

A QUICK HELLO (AS I KNOW YOU'RE BUSY KEEPING YOUR TINY HUMAN ALIVE)

Dear Every Mum,

No matter how you give birth; no matter how you feed your tiny human; no matter if you are a co-sleeper, a breast-feeder, a baby sling wearer, a baby-led weaner, a home-grown organic mum, a home-opened fish finger mum, a gentle parenting mum, a 'Get your shoes on RIGHT NOW before I turn into the Hulk' mum, a stay-at-home mum, a back-to-work mum, an 'I'm not getting dressed today' mum, a mum struggling with her mental health, a mum feeling judged, or a mum feeling on top of the world . . .

NO. MATTER. WHAT. You, *my gorgeous and magnificent new friend,* deserve the right to enjoy motherhood.

A TINY WORD FROM MY TINY HUMANS

A little like trying to get through a HOT drink of anything nowadays, I similarly, couldn't get through the intro of this book, without my tiny humans sharing their thoughts on it all. Over to you girls . . .

MUMMY'S STARTING A REVOLUTION

Our mummy doesn't like it when people say unkind things about other mums. She says this is being judgmental and that no mummy deserves that.

Our mummy thinks it's very important to tell the truth, no matter how hard it may be. She believes that not telling fibs about what being a mummy is really like will make other mummies feel better about themselves and not like they are the only one going through it.

Mummy is not scared about telling the truth.

She was once, though. When she first became a mum, our mummy thought she wasn't doing a good enough job, that everyone else was doing better at it than her, but she was too scared to talk about it. She felt alone and not very brave. She was scared to tell the truth that sometimes being a mummy is hard and that it sometimes made her think unkind things about herself.

Our mummy soon learnt that telling the truth about her experiences of being a mummy, even the more difficult parts about her mind getting poorly, helped other mummies share their experiences. And that made her and other mummies feel less alone and more brave.

Our mummy really cares about this book and the people who read it. She doesn't want to sound corny or like something she calls a 'prom queen', but she really wants to make a difference with what she has written and help bring together other mummies who also believe in being kind to other mums.

Our mummy wants to create a big group of these mums all showing support rather than judgement to each other, even if these mums do things differently.

So Mummy has made a decision.

Mummy's starting a revolution.

The Every Mum Revolution, supporting EVERY mum – NO judgement!

She would love you to join her.

Love Éva-Loren & Isla-Mai

CHAPTER 1

BULLS***

OK, so have I got your attention?

I hope so, because I have a feeling in my knackered, mummy bones (without being too presumptuous, as we have only just met) that we are going to be great friends. You know the kind. The kind who, after just five minutes and five swigs of fizzy wine, are sharing life stories, birth trauma, sex-gone-wrong tales and the fact our bikini lines are less Brazilian, more *Gorillas in the Mist* since pushing a tiny human out. Yes, THAT type of friendship; the type we all dream about and seldom have the pleasure or fortune to have in our new mum-shaped lives.

You and me, I want us to be that type of friend – and like any good, no, GREAT friendship, we need to agree that the things we share between these pages (and what happened between our legs) is, of course, just between us.

Deal?

Can I take it from you silently nodding your head that means you are in?

BRILLIANT!

So, now you've managed to stash your tiny human somewhere to get a few minutes peace to read this book, let me introduce myself properly.

My name is Liv. I am the often bedraggled, occasionally ferocious protector of two tiny humans. I am also a writer. The writer bit came second as, before motherhood, I was a closet writer. Which meant, I didn't have the literary balls to show my work to anyone. However, once I'd shown my vagina to a bunch of strangers (thanks to the beauty of childbirth, not me being a porn star), showing something I'd written to the world was no longer as terrifying as my brain first had me believe (who'd a thunk it?!). Motherhood, for this (and for other unforgettable gifts such as permanent piles, sleepless nights, an uncontrollable bladder, oh, and my two beautiful tiny humans) I thank you.

So, what else can I tell you?

Oh yes, I'm knackered and a little bit mental. Officially, I am the first (knackered) all of the time and have been the second (mental) some of the time. Just to clarify, when I say 'mental' I don't mean the cool London-meets-LA speak 'mental'. You know the 'Yeah, my life is SO fooking MENTAL since having kids, I'm like, SO CRAZY'. No. I actually mean, full on, officially diagnosed by a doctor, mental. All thanks to a visit from those two petrifying and incredibly nasty friends, postnatal depression and postpartum psychosis. But more of this delightfully messed-up tale later. (If you are a lover of horror stories and can't bear the suspense, then feel free to skip the next bit and dive straight into the darkness on page 95).

So, what can I tell you about me on the mum front?

Well for one, I insanely bloody LOVE my tiny humans (two beautiful little girls bursting with character, kindness, snot and glorious sloppy kisses in equal measure) with an unashamed, unbashful and unrelenting ferociousness like no other I've known. It is fair to say that I would singlehandedly slay any fool who gets in my way of loving, providing and protecting them. (I know I sound scary; in real life I actually hate confrontation – honest.) Now, don't get me wrong: like any other good mum out there, I'm not too proud – no, scrap that, I AM proud enough to admit that they also drive me bat-shit-like-a-box-of-frogs-on-speed BONKERS. I love the chaos (most days). I love and hate equally the edges of despair and the precipices of near disasters that I'm teetering on the edge of on an hourly basis thanks to motherhood. And whether or not I have my head together to deal with these days, usually depends on the amount of sleep I haven't had, the number of cataclysmic tantrums I've diffused pre 8 a.m., and if I've ran out of my dry shampoo (which, I've come to realise, is my only real ally when the *Don't kid yourself that you can leave the house looking like that* crap hits the fan).

Now, I know that you're also busy keeping your part of the human race alive (great job, by the way). So, before we get to crack open the fizzy wine and dive into my knackered mummy soul and the rest of this book, I need to first let you in on a little something. After all, any woman worth her salt knows that the only way to cement a great friendship is with a dirty great confession (or two).

So, here goes:

I haven't got a clue what I am doing.

Not one.

SERIOUSLY.

Yes, I am a mother of two tiny humans. And yes, most days I am scared out of my tiny mind that I am making the mother of all mess-ups and that I will ruin their lives forever. And, if I'm really honest, I do not have a scooby doo how I veer from one day to the next, with both my tiny humans still happy (ish), still healthy (ish) and still alive (def more than ish).

Fact.

Wow, it feels better to get that off my chest – thanks!

Since becoming a mum, I've found that telling the truth, no matter how ugly, disgusting or ridiculous a light it paints you in, makes you feel better. And it makes every other mum feel so much better too. Which got me asking: Why on earth do we all seem so hell bent on hiding this truth when it comes to our own experiences of mother-hood?

This leads me nicely to my next confession (I'm on a roll here and I've got a feeling due to the fact you are still with me and haven't put me down to go buy a Kit-Kat or put a wash on that our Every Mum friendship is well on its way to being cemented good and proper). If not the next bit should do the trick…

So here goes, confession No 2:

I don't always enjoy motherhood.

I know. SHOCK HORROR! Right?

I can hear the perfect parenting vigilantes running down the road shouting 'Burn the witch!' right now.

However, isn't this what we all need to hear? Doesn't every mum need to hear the honest truth that motherhood, like everything we turn our hand to in life and similar to everything we experience (even the most magical) isn't always enjoyable all of the time? And that it is totally OK to feel this way. In fact, totally normal and it doesn't mean you're a witch or a terrible mum.

Yes. I know. Big, HUGE confession to make so early in our friendship. Bear with me and I'll tell all.

You see, pre-motherhood I had this image of the mum I was going to be and the sort of motherhood I was going to have. It was the type of motherhood I'd read about in all the magazines and on all the blogs and had seen in films. In my Perfect Mummy mind's eye, I was happy, confident and in total control of this ship called *Mother*. Breezing through my new mum life, creating a perfect home, running a successful new baby business (because that's what all new mums do right?), clad in white linen with a smiley and easy-going baby attached effortlessly to my hip and me enjoying every second of it.

But then, something happened. I pushed a tiny human out of my vagina, and ever since I've noticed a distinct smell of something quite different in the air.

Do you smell it too?

Since becoming a mum do you also feel surrounded by a distinct smell of shit? I do. And, the smell, my lovely new friend, is not coming from my tiny human's nappy or the Poo Pants of Shame I stuffed in my nappy bag three weeks postpartum after accidentally pooing myself in the middle of Mothercare. (Cheers, Mother Nature, for the heads-up that childbirth runs amok with more than just your bladder).

Oh no, that smell burning in my nostrils following the birth of my first tiny human, was the distinct smell of judgmental bullshit being flung at me and other mums from every direction and sucking the joy out of my experience of motherhood. From how I was handling my pregnancy to how I gave birth. Was I bottle-feeding or breast-feeding? Was I a baby wearer? A co-sleeper? A gentle parent? A dummy lover? A baby-lead weaner? To just when exactly was my tiny human planning to crawl, walk, talk, start applying for MENSA!

And you know what? It made me sad. It made me angry. It made me want to do something!

This book in your hands is me Doing Something.

It is me making a stand for every mum out there and saying enough, is enough. Stop with all the perfect parenting propaganda. Stop with all the pressure to be the perfect mum. Stop with all the judgement thrown at mums trying to make the best decisions for themselves and their families. Just please STOP with all the perfect parenting nonsense. Please!

Instead, this book is about bathing in the beauty of own our truth. It is about us being brave. It is about owning our own crazy, beautiful, challenging, dirty, hilarious, disgusting and honest mum reality. It is us telling the world that we are mums who sometimes get it right. We are mums who sometimes make mistakes. We are mums who sometimes have our life together. We are mums who sometimes want to run away from our responsibilities like we are running from a burning building. We are mums who sometimes suffer with our mental health. We are mums who sometimes look hot and we are mums who sometimes just look like we have peeled ourselves off the local park bench after being run over by a herd of snot-wielding tiny humans. However, this is us. This is who we are. No smoke and mirrors, no airbrushing.

For every mum out there feeling lost in the wilderness of motherhood. For every mum out there feeling pressure to be the perfect mum. For every mum out there questioning why their life does not look like the parenting described in the media. For every mum suffering with their mental health. For every mum feeling like they are alone. For every mum questioning if they are a good enough mum. For every mum feeling judged. *This book is for you!*

I want to show every mum that you are good enough. That you are doing a good job. That regardless of whatever is going on with you right this second that you are one hell of a mum and a woman. You are magnificent. Yes, just as you are. No matter how long it's been since you last washed your hair. No matter how short your temper is because you haven't had more than two hours of goddam sleep. No matter how imperfect and inadequate you feel when measured up against your pre-baby vision of how life as a mum *should* be. Just you hold on to this fact: you are already the perfect mum for your glorious, milk-scented, chubby-legged tiny human and regardless of what motherhood throws at you:

You BLOODY ROCK!

Welcome, my friend, to the every mum revolution.

Hold on to your stitches and nappy bags; it's going to be one hell of a ride!

CHAPTER 2

IT'S TIME TO GO BACK . . . WAAAY BACK

So, seeing as you are still with me and haven't been put off by my Poo Pants of Shame confession, I think it's safe to say we are now buddies, amigos, mates, gal pals and fellow Every Mum allies. Therefore, there's only one thing for it. It's time for a Craig David 'Re-Rewind' moment to cement some fellow mum history between these sheets and find out how this mum came to think she was capable of taking care of a tiny human, let alone writing a book about it.

SHE'LL BE COMING ROUND THE MOUNTAIN WHEN SHE COMES

Being pregnant, living up a mountain in a foreign country miles away from my family and the things I cared about most in this world (namely my mum and Boots the Chemist) was not something I ever imagined when I used to flirt with the rose-tinted idea of becoming a mum in my mid-twenties.

Now, don't get me wrong, this isn't as treacherous or as exotic as it may first appear. The mountain was in France, not the Himalayas. It's not as though we were living in a mountainside shack, miles away from civilisation – even though sometimes, when everything in the village shut down between the hours of 12 noon and 2 p.m. and I couldn't go to the supermarket twenty-four hours a day it could feel like it. (Wow! Talk about First World problems!) No, it was France and the Alps – a ski resort called Morzine, to be exact. It was one of the most beautiful places I've ever lived and had fresh running water and an amazing health care system (albeit a ride down the mountain – the hospital not the running water).

So how the hell did I end up here I can hear you asking?

Let's start at the beginning, shall we, and meet the pre-baby me. Let's take a good, long look at her so we can see how far the *free as a bird* mighty have fallen. Hang on a second, I think I can hear her shiny Geneva heels clicking down the shiny Geneva pavement now, clicking and swooshing her way to a swanky client meeting in a swanky Swiss building. (I know, I almost can't believe this me actually existed either!)

So, I know what you're thinking, how the hell did the now disheveled and slightly unhinged me find herself once upon a time clicking down a shiny Swiss high street in shiny Swiss heels?

Well, it went a little something like this. My hubby, Jamie, had lived in France since a teenager and after I went on a ski holiday in his French hometown of Morzine, we were properly Cilla Blacked and hooked up by mutual friends. We were smitten from the word go – or should I say smitten from the first of many drunken snogs as we tried (and failed) to ski home from an end-of-season party on the slopes. The holiday and the snogging ended and I returned back to my life and career in marketing back in the UK. (Yes, I once was a functioning member of society who had a pretty successful career under her belt.) However, six months of long-distance dating later, I'd packed up my career, said goodbye to my City Girl bachelorette pad, hung up my heels and moved to the mountains to be with the boy of my dreams. Bang! No messing! In for a penny, in for a pound – or, as it transpired, a wedding and two tiny humans!

Our life together in France was pretty damn sweet. It was one of doing whatever the hell we wanted, snowboarding, skiing, hanging out with friends, boozy picnics by the lake, and road trips to Italy for lunch that turned into a weekend away. We were carving out a life together that was universes away from my daily commute, 9–5 city life back in the UK. (I could poke my old self bang in the eye right about now: I had NO bloody clue how good I'd got it!)

Now, don't get me wrong, I am a city girl at heart; I love the dirt, the noise and the bristling energy on which a city thrives. However, this new life in the Alpine mountains, was one of adventure, great food, freedom and possibility, all shared with the love of my life. The downside was that I really missed my family. We are a really close bunch – like *EastEnders* close – which drives me bonkers at times when it becomes more dramatic than an *EastEnders* storyline – but I wouldn't be without them. And as they were only a short plane ride away; I went back regularly and they came out to see us when they could.

After a year and a half together (living together and working together on his online ski holiday business), Jamie dragged me out on a snowy walk, bent down on one knee in waist-deep snow and proposed to me in front of our favourite waterfall. (Yes, this place I now found myself living in was so ridiculous we actually had enough choice of waterfalls to class one as our favourite!) A year later, we were married in a beautiful château in front of all our most favourite people, followed by the mother of all parties that rocked le château well into the early hours.

Following the wedding and honeymoon, I landed myself a marketing job in Geneva, earning more money than I'd ever earned or could earn back in the UK. I somehow managed to convince my employer that I should only work four days a week (and one of those from home), and, not surprisingly, we were loving life thanks to the much-coveted disposable income. If it helps, I now want to run back in time and throttle my old self for thinking this type of life and financial freedom would go on forever, even after having babies – pah, fool! So there we were, happily married, with good jobs and living in a beautiful place. It was inevitable that sooner or later talk of tiny humans started to pop up.

GETTING PREGNANT

We'd been really open about both wanting a family from pretty early on, and knew that once we were married we'd want a family of our own. However, it was my hubby who was the first one to suggest that we actively stopped *not* trying for a baby. I still remember where we were when he first said that he thought it was time: a karaoke bar. We were on a six-week trip to Vietnam – our postponed honeymoon that I'd also managed to wangle before starting my new job (seriously, I love Geneva) – drinking way too many two-for-one mojitos and about to be taken to a club by a member of the Vietnam mafia and his security guards. Yes, I said mafia! #bloodyidiots (us, not the mafia).

I turned to him like he was a loon, looking at where we were right then and trying to imagine our life with a baby in it, and told him I wasn't sure. (No shit Sherlock! You were about to go clubbing with the mafia. How the hell was a tiny human going to fit into those plans?) Life-changing conversation over, we then proceeded to do the final shot, sing one last rendition of Jessie J's 'Price Tag' (It's all about the money money money) and went clubbing with our well-connected new friends.

However, after he had planted the reality of a baby in my mind (and the mother of all hangovers had worn off), it grew from a ridiculous idea to an exciting butterfly in my tummy that developed into something we both wanted – and we started *not* not trying for the rest of the trip. I found myself googling 'ovulation calculators' from our dodgy hotel in Ho Chi Min City whilst planning our next stopover, and daydreaming of going home pregnant and ready, after six weeks of adventures, to start the next chapter of our lives (because life is always that textbook, right?).

The idea of being a mum – of going from the two of us to the three of us – went from being a drunken conversation to something I couldn't stop thinking about.

With a mix of naivety and a sprinkle of pre-baby arrogance, I believed that deciding to have a baby meant that we would start trying and, bam, we would be pregnant. I blame the crap sex education we received in Year 9. You see, when us girls are growing up, we are full of fear that we only have to see an erect penis and we will be with child. That unprotected sex leads us on a one-way street to either STDs or pregnancy (both terrifying destinations aged 16). And we grow up safe in the knowledge that one day when we decide, we will become mothers to deliciously chubby and healthy tiny humans and continue to have as many as we want until we decide to call time on our ovaries once we've reached our perfect number of children.

What we are not told is that in fact there is only a small window of opportunity each month to get pregnant. That our biology and cycles have to be aligned to ensure it's possible for us to get pregnant. That even once we become pregnant the journey our tiny human has to complete to finally end up safe, healthy and in our arms can be so precarious that some don't make it or if they do are not able to stay with us for long. We don't realise that our ovaries may have already called time on us, long before we even decided we are ready to become a mum. It's bloody terrifying to realise that something we are programmed to believe is our natural right as a woman – to grow and bring a tiny human into this world – may not be our right after all. That our bodies, despite being in good physical condition, are not able to produce the one thing we want most in the world.

So back to me and my foolish notion that we would get pregnant purely because we were on our honeymoon and I was off the pill. I missed a period a couple of weeks before coming back from the trip, we got overly excited – only to do a test and taste the first taste of disappointment, a taste with a strength that amazed us. A few weeks earlier, we hadn't even known we wanted a baby. Now, we'd spoken about it, and it was all we wanted. We ended up shrugging this off and calmly chastising ourselves for thinking it would have happened so quickly, but also being happy that it proved to us without a shadow of a doubt how much we wanted this little person in our lives.

This calm nonchalance was all well and good at the start. However, once the months started to tick by, without a blue line making an appearance, we started to worry. We both told each other it was crazy; it had only been a few months and we knew rationally that it could take up to a year or longer. But we still couldn't stop the little niggling of fear of 'What if it isn't going to happen for us?' and 'What if there is something wrong with one of us?'.

I'd heard about ovulation sticks from family and friends, but I didn't know if this was the right way to go about things or just let things happen naturally. This worry was compounded by a remark someone said to me when we were talking about couples 'actively trying' for a baby and using these sticks to help them know the best time to be having sex: 'Oh, I would hate to do that. To be one of those couples who have to have sex even if they don't want to, just to have a baby. I'd much rather just go with the flow and see what happens.'

My response to this?

BULLSHIT!

Give yourself a couple of months of 'just seeing what happens' and, when nothing does, of feeling the anxiety start to build along with the fear that it may not 'just happen' for you, that you may not be lucky enough to have the baby you've been dreaming about. Give yourself a couple of months of that and then tell me what you think about increasing your chances of conceiving by knowing the optimum time to get pregnant thanks to weeing on a stick? Anyone who has ever tried for a baby knows that once you get a few failed months under your unfastened chastity belt you will try ANYTHING to get with child – from having sex on the smiley days even when you are feeling more knackered than turned on to trying more 'effective' positions and the waiting with yours leg in the air after having sex. Literally ANYTHING. And you know what? So, you should. There is no shame in it, nothing to feel embarrassed or unnatural about trying anything you can to get pregnant, even peeing on a stick.

Therefore, never feel ashamed or embarrassed about whatever route you take to being able to bring your tiny human into this world – and, most importantly, never feel judged on it. Never!

FINDING OUT WE WERE PREGNANT

So, these Bad Boy ovulation sticks worked a treat and after a couple of months of using them along with every other Old Wives' trick in the book, we were officially in the club. However, thanks to me being crap at calculating my cycle dates – or, if I'm honest, anything mathematical (sorry, Mr Warton, all that GCSE maths tuition never really stuck!) – I didn't realise I was late until almost a week afterwards! Oh yes, thanks to me miscounting the days on my work calendar, I was nearly a week late, and the smell of coffee (hard to escape when working in an office in Geneva because it runs through the veins of these people) was making me want to throw up during every meeting. In true Swiss fashion, we had a lot of meetings and a lot of coffee.

So, there I was at my desk in Geneva, when it struck me that I might have miscalculated. I started to recount the days and yes, yes, divvy here had made a mistake. My stomach somersaulted (not just because of the reek of coffee) as I dared to let myself believe that I might have a little person already growing inside me. I reached for my phone and called my hubby straightaway.

'I think I'm five days late.'

He was so excited, and we both couldn't wait to get home so we could do the test together. So there we were, hours later, at home surrounded by a wide-grinned bubble of nervous energy wanting it so much to be true. Not quite believing it could be and trying to hold onto our heads and our hearts in case the lines did not appear – or, in the case of our French digital Clear Blue test, the word *enceinte* did not appear.

It was the longest few minutes of our lives. I did the test, saw the timer start and was so scared to keep looking at it that we placed it on the coffee table, out of sight and out of reach, and sat on the sofa together like two bunnies in the headlights, grinning and giggling at each other like loons.

'Shall we look?'

'No, it won't have worked yet.'

'The timer's still going.'

'Stop looking.'

'OK.'

'Stop peeking at it, I can see you looking, come and sit back down.'

'Oh my God, do you think we could be?'

'I don't know, do you?'

'What if it's positive, can you imagine?'

More grinning like loons.

'Do you feel like you are?'

'Yes. No. Oh God, I don't know!'

'Shit, we really could be pregnant!'

Fingers crossed harder than ever before.

'Right, time's up. What should we do?'

'You look.'

'No, you look.'

'OK.'

'Wait! Let's look together.'

'OK.'

And there it was for the world to see: *Enceinte – 3–4 semaines*.

We were pregnant. We were three to four weeks pregnant. It had only bloody worked!

We both stood in the middle of our lounge, clutching the test stick, clutching each other and crying tears of disbelief and happiness.

We couldn't stop staring at each other in wide-eyed disbelief, fast calculating the due date to be sometime in late January, hugging each other, minds blown that there were now three of us sat together on the sofa, and wondering: When would I start showing? When we should go to the doctor? Would it be a boy or a girl? So many questions, so many emotions, so many exciting times ahead of us. A whole new world. A world we had no idea about.

Those first moments finding out we were going to be parents, that we were going to bring another being into the world, reminded me of how I feel when looking into the vastness of the night sky, so enormous, so unexplainable and breathtakingly beautiful. We were staring into the face of a miracle no words or thoughts could explain or even begin to contain.

So what do you do when faced with such a miracle? Well, if you're greedy beggars like us, you get your asses out for a slap-up mountain dinner, of course! So, we packed ourselves and our new beautiful little secret into the car and went to a remote mountainside restaurant, where we were guaranteed not to bump into anyone we knew (word travels fast in a mountain village) and were therefore able to talk freely about our new little person and start making plans for our future as a family of three.

BRING IT ON!

CHAPTER 3

PREGNANT AND BLOOMING – (AKA BLOOMING DEMONIC, STARVING AND WILLING TO KILL FOR A CHEESE BURGER AND A FULL-FAT COKE)

Those weeks when we carried around our secret really were magical. Just the two of us, feeling excited and special, sharing the baby whilst the rest of the world was unawares. We went to the doctor and he assigned us a gynaecologist (down the mountain). We already knew of him thanks to his God-like status; he had delivered most of the babies in our village. My mates and I used to joke about how the same man had seen all our fannies! Bit crude maybe, but hey, when you're pregnant and not drinking you have to get your kicks somewhere right?

MORNING SICKNESS – AKA FEELING CONSTANTLY HUNGOVER MINUS THE FUN OF GETTING INAPPROPRIATELY SMASHED!

Boy, oh boy, do we need these kicks when the all-day, 'When is this going to end?' morning sickness kicks in.

Oh yes, along came the seven weeks pregnant mark, bringing its stomach-turning mate with him, and so ensued six weeks of me feeling worse than I did the morning after drinking my body weight in Jaegar with the Vietnamese mafia. Oh and not to forget me looking radiant and blooming aka stuffing my face with Fizzy Haribo, Cheese Burgers and full fat Coke under a blanket on the sofa whenever I got the chance.

God, it was hell (not the stuffing my face obvs that was pretty, darn special). The sickness. Ugghhhh! My early pregnancy days consisted of peeling myself out of bed and wanting to puke or crumble into smithereens of exhaustion (usually both). And then having to get my sorry-for-myself ass ready to face the long and winding drive down the mountain and then across the border into Switzerland. All whilst switching between wanting to suck the life out of orange segments to wanting to puke up in the plastic carrier bag I now carried as a staple accessory on the passenger seat.

So, as you can imagine the last thing I felt at nine weeks pregnant was sociable! And I so wish someone at the time had told me it was OK to want to cocoon myself away from the world, to be able to come home, put on my fat bum pants and flake – after a day of fooling the rest of the outside world that I was feeling my usual normal self. If you are currently pregnant and wanting to do nothing more than sit on your gorgeous pregnant bottom and chill out, then guess what? You can! Now, go get your stretchy telly pants on, get horizontal and enjoy every moment of it, my lovely.

I was not prepared mentally for the level of emotions and exhaustion I felt. I had brought into the 'I'm not sick, I'm just pregnant' malarkey and was determined to carry on as normal despite just wanting to rest. No one had told me to ease off the pressure, to allow myself to be pregnant and tired and to know that this is OK. This is normal.

Without this little nugget of advice, my hubby had to learn the hard way of what it is like to cross swords with a knackered creator of human life.

One evening, I was feeling like total and utter dog turd thanks to the morning sickness. I'd spent the day at work pretending I was on top of my game to all my work colleagues whilst taking sneaky naps in the staff loos. I'd finally made it home after a particularly stomach-churning and exhausting drive home up the winding mountain roads, which had me dry-retching at every bend like a rabid dog. I walked into the house desperate to get into my PJs and onto the sofa, bury my face into my standard bag of Haribo, when my darling hubby reminded me that, there were other plans afoot: I now had to get my glad rags on because we were leaving in ten minutes to go for dinner with friends.

WTF?

I had no words. Literally not even one bloody syllable.

However, I did have huge, ugly, face-distorting, snot-dripping sobs, and proceeded to soak him, the kitchen floor and anything within three feet of me with them.

The look on my hubby's face was priceless. Like some weird bug-eyed, snot-a-whalling creature had just slithered her way in, pretending to be his wife. (He had no idea what was yet to come!)

Bewildered and fearing for his life, he dared to approach and try to convince me that it would be a good and enjoyable thing to go out for dinner with our friends.

He might as well have been inviting me to dine with Satan himself whilst sat on a pile of upturned drawing pins.

Now obviously, he was not growing body parts, so he couldn't quite get his head around either my hysterics or the levels of unadulterated exhaustion and irrationality. As far as he was concerned, I had just finished work for the week and we could now look forward to a lovely night with our friends. However, for knackered and pregnant me, it was the end of my sofa-obsessed world. I'd driven to and from a different country to get to work, whilst trying not to puke my guts up on the mountainside or at the border control. Then I'd faced a long day of meetings talking about internal ad campaigns, meeting agendas and newsletters; endured a team meeting where everyone stank of coffee and fags; listened until my brain hurt trying to fathom out what everyone was saying in their lightning speed French – all whilst wanting to crawl under my desk, puke in the plant pot and take a nap on my colleague Jean-Luc's discarded and very expensive laptop bag. I'd kept up the farcical charade that all was well, I was 'fine', on top of the world and my job.

Now the thought of having to continue the pretence and lie to my good friends, to desperately think of a believable excuse as to why I was not drinking my usual Friday night gallon of vin blanc whilst watching everyone else get pissed – when all I wanted to do was put on my elasticated PJ bottoms, curl up under a blanket and stuff my face with anything that would stop this nausea – was all just too much for this pregnant lady to take.

After more sobbing and some demonic grunts from my good self, the pregnancy penny finally dropped and my hubby realised that holy hell, he was actually talking to his wife who was now pregnant, overtired, overemotional and wanting to puke and then sleep for a billion years. With his life hanging in the balance, he got the message, tucked me up on the sofa and went to dinner armed with apologies and excuses for me not being able to make it. The moral of this story? Listen to yourself and do what's best for you. You ARE allowed.

PREGNANCY CAN BE BLOODY SCARY

All was going well with my pregnancy. I felt like dog turd most of the time, but I'd read on one of the baby websites now bombarding me with emails, that it was a good sign to feel so ill. Then, at around seven weeks, we had the shock of our lives: I noticed I was bleeding. I felt sick and devastated, immediately thinking the worst. We phoned our doctor, who reassured us that this can be normal at this stage, but we wanted to go into hospital just to be on the safe side. The hospital was an hour away down the mountain (I was now beginning to curse the fact we were so far away!) and it became one of the longest drives of our lives. We drove most of the way in silence, not daring to voice our fears that the little person we had been secretly planning and celebrating was being taken away from us. We tried to fill that hour with reassuring words, but the fear in the air of our car was palpable.

Once we got to the hospital and were ushered into our room, the nurse explained she was going to do a scan and see if she could find a heartbeat. I felt sick, panicked and couldn't dare let my mind wonder: What if she can't?

They were long and terrifying minutes as she smothered my un-pregnant-looking tummy with cold jelly and then proceeded to look for the baby and any sign of a tiny heart beat. She assured us that she was having trouble finding it only because the pregnancy was so early. Then she pressed down harder and bingo, she found it! We were relieved for a millisecond – until she informed us that she was worried that it was very faint and told us that we'd have to come back in a week's time.

Faint? What the hell did that mean? Did she know something we didn't and was holding out on us? Was there something wrong and we were going to find out the full extent of how wrong at the next scan? I wanted to scream at her for not giving us the reassurance that everything was OK! I knew that it wasn't her fault and that she had to be as matter-of-fact as possible with us, but I could have swung at her for being so black and white and unemotional with us.

So, relieved and worried sick all at the same time, we left the hospital and somehow got through the next week, worrying that any little twinge meant something sinister – and worrying even more if I didn't feel as sick as I thought I should be or had been a few days prior. Thankfully one week and another scan later we got the news we had been longing for: so far, all was OK with our baby and the heartbeat was now normal for the time in its pregnancy. We left the hospital clutching the scan picture of our alien-like but perfectly normal tiny human and cried with relief and happiness all the way back up the mountain. Now, we thought, we could get on with the rest of the pregnancy, knowing the baby was healthy.

However, the night before our twelve-week scan, I started to bleed heavily. This made our previous scare seem like nothing. It was dinnertime when it happened, and in despair and blind panic we called the hospital to see what we should do. 'Nothing' was their pragmatic, black and white response. I was advised to stay where I was, to take it easy, and monitor the bleeding – and, if I started to get severe pains, to go straight in. The harsh and heartbreaking reality was that if I was having a miscarriage, then medically there was nothing they could do to stop it. We would have no choice but to let nature run its course. So, we did. I sat there numb, with my feet up on a cushion (thinking this would help keep the baby where it should be), not daring to move, just waiting to see what happened. Since we had our twelve-week scan booked for the following day, I knew I just had to sit tight, keep calm and hope beyond hope that everything was going to be OK.

We arrived the next morning, grim-faced, racked with anxiety and fearing the worst – and got to see why our gynaecologist was held in such God-like esteem. As soon as we told him what had happened the night before, he cut our conversations short and whisked me into the scan room. Before I knew what was happening or had any time to worry further, he had the probe on my tummy and a heartbeat booming out on high volume around the room.

'C'est bon!' – 'It's fine'

I could have French kissed that French man right there and then in front of my hubby and my unborn child. Happy, relieved, over the moon – none of that comes even close to the delight that I felt. And this wasn't only to do with the obvious and overwhelming relief that our baby was OK and had survived another scare, but also the way in which he dealt with the whole situation. No messing about, no long lingering wait to find the heartbeat, no doubt-filled seconds of dread. Just bang, boom, everything fine!

Our tiny human was only twelve weeks in creation and was already causing heart-stopping drama and keeping us well and truly on our toes. We were soon to find out this would follow us into later pregnancy and out into the real world. (More of this little beauty later!)

IT'S NOT 'C'EST BON' FOR EVERYONE

I hope you don't mind, but I'd like to take a little pause here to pay respect to those mums and dads who don't get the news they are longing to hear about their tiny humans. Who don't get to feel the relief the words 'everything's normal' brings. Whose scares are not just scares but are instead warning signs that something is terribly wrong or that their little person is having to leave them. I want to honour all the precious tiny humans who are no longer with us, and show my love and respect to all the mums, dads and families who have suffered.

** Anyone needing support after going through child bereavement please see the list of support services detailed in the back of the book on page 236

TRYING AND FAILING TO KEEP UP THE 'I'M NOT PREGNANT!' CHARADE!

I think one of the most exhausting things when you first become pregnant (alongside the raging hormones and zapping of energy due to your body performing its very own hidden miracle) is the whole bloody effort of keeping it hidden from your nearest and dearest. I have no idea what I was thinking when I concocted my own tall tales of 'I'm not pregnant bullshit', but wow, they were pretty special.

I took my big pregnancy cover-up to epic proportions. You see, not quite satisfied with the bog standard and tried-and-tested cover-ups used by millions of pregnant ladies before me – 'I'm on antibiotics', 'I'm on a detox', 'I'm the designated driver' etc., etc. – I instead concocted such a ridiculous tale that not even I was convinced by it. Now, before we carry on with this, I'm going to apologise to you right now for how much you are going to cringe throughout the next section and also question (probably not for the first or the last time) how much level of crazy and downright idiotic one person can be. Read on, my friend, read on . . .

So, there I was, pregnant and coming from the school of thought that the more detail and extravagant the story, the more likely people were to believe it. Right? Especially since, as far as my good friends were concerned, me turning down booze at a party, a dinner or, let's face it, anything even slightly like a social gathering was like me refusing to breathe. Therefore, my thinking was that it had to be something quite dramatic for them to believe me. (I am aware now that I sound like a total boozehound.)

So the storyteller in me set out to weave her tall and incredibly shit tales. Tales that involved me blurting out to anyone and everyone who even made the slightest suggestion that I may want a drink or to consume a slightly undercooked anything: 'I have parasites.'

Oh yes, that old chestnut.

Seriously, what was I thinking?

And why the hell did my poor hubby go along with it? (Oh yes, dear friends, I took him down with me too.)

There we would be, throughout those first twelve weeks of pregnancy, attending BBQs, birthday parties and dinners out with friends. Me and my hubby side by side and nodding in unison as I proclaimed for the billionth time that 'Yes, the reason I am not drinking is because I have parasites!' All whilst my friends, acquaintances, and sometimes people I'd never even met before looked at me with a mix of bemusement and what can only be described as mild disgust as they imagined me being riddled with these parasites running amok around my body and stopping me from drinking. I mean, come on, why the hell would having parasites stop me from drinking? It's fair to say that pregnancy had driven me slightly cuckoo.

Luckily, most people who heard this tall and ever so slightly odd tale seemed convinced enough – or, at least slightly disgusted or embarrassed enough – not to probe deeper. Instead, they would back away from me slowly whilst taking a big gulp from the glass of wine they had been offering to me. That is, until one day, when I found myself at another BBQ (damn being pregnant during good weather months!), turning down rosé coming at me from every direction and spinning the same bullshit yarn about my bloody parasites to everyone.

I'd gotten quite good at it, too. Like any good storyteller, I was dedicated to my craft and had embellished it as the weeks had past. These imaginary parasites had now become something I'd picked up whilst travelling around Vietnam and which had laid dormant until now to attack with a vengeance. Poor old me, eh.

Usually this was the point where my tall tale would stop, the audience satisfied by the amount of detail and, quite frankly, put off by the grossness of it all. But this evening my audience included a nurse.

Oh yes, there I was, telling my fully embellished tale to a medical professional, who after listening carefully to my sorrowful tale and nodding in all the right places, asked: 'Do you really have parasites?'

'Yes, yes I have, bloody awful they are,' I replied, following it with my well practised sigh of acceptance.

'But, what do you mean?'

Oh shit . . . 'Well, I have parasites.'

'Right, but how? Which type?'

Oh shit, shit, shit! 'I can't quite remember the long name for them.' I was starting to unravel. 'I've had blood tests and everything [don't know what the hell I meant by *everything*] and the doctor reckons I picked them up whilst travelling around Vietnam.'

'Right, and where are they these parasites?'

She had me on the run. 'In my bum.' *IN MY BUM?!? MY GOD WHAT THE HELL WAS WRONG WITH ME?* I'd just told someone I'd never met before, in the middle of a summer BBQ, that I had Vietnamese parasites residing in my arsehole. Still, I was determined to keep this long-established cock and bull story on track, so I embellished further, explaining they were sore and itched like hell.

'What and you can't drink because of them?'

There was no let up with this woman! 'No, because I am on antibiotics for them.'

'Oh really? Which ones? I'm a nurse and I could check them for if you want, as you can drink on some of them, you know.'

Sod this! I was in above my head this time, trying to con a medical professional who quite obviously knew her shit and could see through mine. 'I'm pregnant.'

'What?'

'Sorry, I'm pregnant and I just made up all of that rubbish. I don't have parasites. I'm having a baby.'

'Ha, ha, and that's the best story you could come up with?'

'Yes. Yes, I'm afraid it is.' Hangs head in shame.

Game, set, match to the inquisitive medical professional.

Luckily, this switched-on and shrewd nurse soon went on to become one of my best mates and it turns out she was pregnant too (minus the shit cover-up story). She was already at the twelve-week stage, so all this making up of tall tales to convince people you were the carrier of parasites rather than a baby was now behind her.

Needless to say it was a bloody relief to finally get to tell everyone.

'I'M NOT SICK, I'M JUST PREGNANT'

So, I have been pregnant for a grand total of two times. Both pregnancies were such polar opposites that it made me realise that pregnancy can be wonderful (as it was with my first), but it can also totally screw you over (as it did with my second, me lying on my hippo-sized arse unable to do anything for fear of the baby coming prematurely). Who knew that bringing life into this world can be a wonderful, sun shining, birds singing, blooming in the face of the world experience one time and the next time make you feel so awful that you never want to do it again?

I have to admit I was a smug pregnant biatch with my first tiny human. So much so that the thought of me bounding along with my neat bump, glossy pregnancy hair, glowing skin and full of energy, chanting the motto of 'I'm not sick, I'm just pregnant', made my second-time pregnant self want to go back in time and punch my smug self in my smug face.

After the passing of the morning sickness in my first pregnancy, I felt great. I was full of energy and optimism. I exercised three times a week, and had a personal pregnancy yoga instructor who had me and bump doing shoulder stands. My hair and skin looked the best it ever had, I was full of life in every sense of the word, and so, so excited about being pregnant and becoming a mum. I can honestly say it was one of the happiest times of my life, when I felt my most calm and purposeful, doing exactly what I was meant to be doing.

You can imagine my shock when my second pregnancy didn't quite follow the same pattern and instead taught me that pregnancy can also be one of the toughest, anxiety-riddled and overwhelming times too. And a time when we are at our most unwell. At just sixteen weeks pregnant with my second tiny human, I was having contractions, suffering from extremely low blood pressure, put on bed rest and signed off work. Oh yes, no yoga head stands for me! Like I said, pregnancy polar opposites!

So, I am going to break the mould here of every baby book that has come before me and say this:

Not every pregnancy is a delight.

You are not guaranteed to have a textbook pregnancy where everything is blooming and glowing in your garden. Sometimes you can have a pregnancy that makes you wish each day away, not to be closer to the day you get to hold your baby, but to be closer to the day where you will no longer feel like death warmed up. I am here to tell you that if you are currently feeling like this or have felt like this, you are not alone. It's OK, you are not the devil just because you don't or didn't enjoy being pregnant.

Pregnancy is also a time when we can start to feel judged on the decisions we make – from what we eat and how we exercise to what type of birth we are planning. This is where I felt the first elements of judgement starting to trickle into my life. What 'type' of pregnant was I going to be? The cool and easy-going pregnant, carrying on as normal, eating what I liked, socialising in flats and not batting a knackered eyelid at being designated driver YET AGAIN? The whingy and precious pregnant, griping about everything from how tired I was to how fat I was getting? The crazy neurotic pregnant, worrying over every little thing, doing everything by the book and not daring to have uncooked meat in the house let alone on my plate? Or the earth mother pregnant, walking barefoot, wafting joss sticks and ensuring an environment of positivity at all times around my growing bump and praying to Aluna, my pregnancy goddess. (Please note I have no idea who Aluna is. Cool name, though. Big shout out to any of you Alunas out there.)

The judgement also seeped into how I looked. Was my bump going to be 'neat and tidy' or more like an out-of-control oil spill in the Pacific, smothering everything in its path? Was I going to look fifty-seven weeks rather than the seventeen weeks I was? Or would bump and I look like a celeb mum rocking the chic bump without the heaven of a maternity legging in sight (I still miss them!)?

I came to realise the sorry (and, quite frankly, disturbing) levels of judgement fired down on pregnant women when I was stopped in the street by someone I barely knew, who proceeded to compliment me on how well I looked (nice) and how tiny my bump was. (Apparently, having a small bump and hardly looking pregnant equates to looking well; seems a bit weird.) Then she started to rip pieces out of another pregnant lady she knew who had 'a massive bump', telling me I should be 'grateful' because I looked so much better than her. WTF? I stood there in shock as one woman ripped into a pregnant woman about how she looked. It was offensive. It was uncalled for. It was a judgemental attack I had not seen since the playground.

I often think this was one of the first instances when I felt an urge to stand up for and protect other mums and mums-to-be. This was the place where my passion and fire was lit in honour of supporting every mum – no judgement. It was an empowering realisation that it is our job as women to lift up our fellow warriors on the battlefield of life rather than to be the ones slaying them and leaving them gurgling facedown in the mud.

The judgement I encountered during both pregnancies, and the huge differences I experienced, has fuelled my belief that us mums need to be prepared for whatever pregnancy throws at us, to ensure that we are not left in a bedraggled state before the hard work really starts – once we've pushed out our tiny humans into the world and life gets real.

Not in any of the pregnancy books that I read, did it ever mention that being pregnant is not always a walk in the park. That at times it can be a bit crap and at other times downright terrifying. That as life-affirming and wonderful and as easy as it can be for some, for others it can be anything but. That not everyone gets the cookie cutter pregnancy described in the media. That, like pregnancy bumps, pregnancy itself comes in all shapes and sizes and we should all be talking about ALL experiences of it (the good, the bad and the scary), to ensure we are all as prepared and as mentally strong as possible for whatever comes our way. Most importantly, we should not be judging other mums but empowering and supporting every mum through their pregnancies.

THE BULLS*** TO IGNORE WHEN PREGNANT

One of the things that always bemused me – and, if I'm honest, felt pressured by – was the amount of opinions laid on me while pregnant. From how I should be acting, feeling and dressing to how big my bump was, to what I should or should not be eating. The list goes on and on and on and on and on until you want to stick your own cankle in your mouth (or theirs) to make them stop!

I wish someone had told me that I didn't have to take it all on board or so personally. That just because advice is offered I didn't have to take it. And that, more importantly, advice is a bit like shoes: you don't have room in your wardrobe for every pair. Some you won't like, and some, which you think will be perfect for you, won't fit at all. Most importantly, sometimes you will say to hell with it all and instead walk barefoot, shoe- and advice-free.

This is what really inspired me to put pen to paper, so that mums-to-be who found themselves in some of the situations I faced during my pregnancies would know they are not alone. That they don't have to give a crap about what anyone else thinks; the only opinion which really matters is their own. It's your pregnancy, your body and your baby, after all!

With that in mind, here is my list of the bullshit to ignore when pregnant:

1. 'Remember you are pregnant, not ill.'

Really? Have you really just said that to my face? To my green around the gills, *If I have to smell a waft of air freshener or whiff another overripe banana I am going to puke my guts up*. Oh, and I should feel grateful should I that I have only twelve weeks of this to endure all whilst pretending that I am fine and bloody dandy? That my boobs don't ache beyond recognition? That my skin is not itching all over like

I am infested with a billion creepy crawlies? That I am rushing to the toilet to dry retch every half-hour? All whilst my brain is on high alert panicking over every slight twinge and my body just wants to wave the white flag and surrender into a crumpled heap on the floor.

Anyone who dares to breathe these words to you whilst pregnant deserves a short, sharp punch in the gut.

2. 'Don't be too precious about yourself.'

WTF? You are growing a human being all on your own. That's right: tiny feet, hands, heart and a brain, to name just a few of the awe-inspiring tasks you are completing on a weekly basis! If anyone deserves to be treated like a precious commodity, it is you and your growing bump! Over the years, the term 'precious' has been used as a derogatory term. 'Ooh, she's a bit precious', 'Ooh, you don't have to be so precious about yourself.' Well I am saying a big up yours to these idiots who dare say this to expectant or new mums.

Taking care of yourself and doing what feels right for you and your bump whilst pregnant is top of your agenda – and to hell with anyone who uses the p-word.

3. 'You have to carry on as normal.'

Normal – are you kidding me? There is nothing normal or day-to-day about harbouring a human stowaway in your body for nine months and then passing it through the eye of a needle that is your vagina. If you feel great and want to go to all the social engagements and gym classes going, fantastic! However, if the thought of keeping up appearances and making out that you feel blooming and bursting with energy is making you want to squeeze lemon onto the backs of your eyeballs, then just say no! Yes, the magic word that evaporates all the responsibilities and hassle of having to get ready in a bump-flattering outfit, paint on a smile and pretend that you wouldn't rather be at home in your PJs, watching *Corrie* and eating chocolate biscuits.

4. 'In my day there was none of this nonsense about what you should and shouldn't be doing when pregnant.'

Yes, but you also had parent and baby books advising you that smoking was OK as long as it was in moderation! Obviously, there are some things that can now seem a bit OTT when it comes to all the things pregnant mums need to remember as out of bounds and harmful to themselves and their growing baby. However, some of these restrictions are there for a valid reason (aka medical advances) and just because they were not around thirty years ago does not mean that they are a scaremongering tactic or that as mums we are being fussy and over-cautious if we abide by them. We are just doing what we have been advised is the best way to bring our baby into this world, so please don't try and make us feel otherwise.

5. 'Once you get that baby in your arms, everything will feel right.'

We all know that we need to keep ourselves fit and well throughout pregnancy, and that we need to prepare for childbirth through regular exercise and good nutrition. However, we don't often take time to ensure we are taking care of our mental wellbeing. We are instead told that, once we become a mum, everything will just feel 'right'. But what do we do if it doesn't?

Both our bodies and our minds go through huge monumental changes whilst we are pregnant, and then when we become mums. Therefore, we need to make sure we take care of our mental health by ensuring that we talk about any anxieties and worries we may have, and by taking time out to rest. We have to make ourselves a priority by educating ourselves on maternal mental health illnesses – what they are and where to get the right help and support if we are suffering through pregnancy or following the birth of our baby. (For anyone needing support during pregnancy or after the birth of your baby then please see pages 236–238 for support services you can access.)

6. 'Ohhh let me have a feel!'

They come at you from out of nowhere. Before you know it, you have a pair of hands feeling and rubbing their way across your stomach whilst you look on in shock and dismay. And as your pregnancy and size of bump progresses, it seems you are fair game for anyone to have a grope. The worst are the totally inappropriate tummy terrorists who think that feeling the lower part of your bump is acceptable rather than verging on sexual harassment. 'Don't you realise your hands are sitting on the top of my vagina! Please get the hell away from me!'

7. 'Wow you're getting big!'

The only comment anyone should pass about the size of your bump or appearance during pregnancy is to tell you how great you look. I don't care if you are the size of a hippo on steroids or are alternatively verging on the smaller side, no one should be passing comment – at least, not out loud and not to your face! Comments such as 'Wow, you're getting big' should be met with 'No shit Sherlock, I'm growing a human. What's your excuse?' And anyone who dares comment, 'Wow you're tiny, are you sure that's normal?' should be met with a kick to the shin.

8. 'When can we come and stay?'

'Hmmmm, you can't!'. Visitors popping in for an hour is one thing. Hopefully, they will come bearing prepared meals and compliments and no expectations of being hosted, and then after whipping the hoover around and washing up their tea cups, they'll be on their merry way. Overnight houseguests you don't have to accept. You have become a mum, not a B & B!

9. 'Oh you're taking the easy way out and having an epidural?'

There is no 'easy way' out when you are trying to push a baby out of a small hole in your body. Fact. As mums-to-be we are bombarded with opinions about how we should be bringing our tiny human into the world, with our options graded from being hardcore and doing it drug-free to taking the easy way out by having an epidural or a C-section. Let me be the first to tell you that all of it is damn hardcore! Each option is challenging and scary as hell. No matter how you bring your tiny human into the world, you are a ROCK STAR!

10. 'So, come on, tell me your baby names.'
DON'T DO IT! Seriously, no matter how strong the urge to spill the beans on the carefully planned names that both you and your partner have fallen in love with, keep them to yourself. Just one slightly off response of 'Oh, really' or 'Wow, that's a bit unusual' will have you backtracking for the rest of your pregnancy.

11. 'Ooh, make the most of your sleep/life/whatever – because when the baby comes, your life is over!'
Just shut the fuck up, will you!

CHAPTER 4

CHILDBIRTH, AKA TRYING TO PUSH A TINY HUMAN OUT OF YOUR VAGINA

THANK GOD FOR ONE BORN EVERY MINUTE!

I have to admit it, before the birth of my first tiny human I didn't pay the actual giving birth bit much attention (STUPIDLY). When I mentioned antenatal groups to my gynaecologist and he realised how long the journey up and down the mountain would take, he told me not to bother, so I didn't! Oh yes, the sheer pre-baby bliss of not knowing what lies ahead and the bloody cruelty of hindsight when I was 5 centimetres dilated, screaming like a demon and wanting to punch the aforementioned gynae in the face for not frogmarching me to those meetings! (Thank God for *One Born Every Minute*, which I watched religiously throughout my first pregnancy.)

Antenatal classes in France don't seem to hold the same importance as they do here in the UK (well, not to my gynaecologist at least). And I have to admit that, despite the horror stories I've heard about antenatal groups from other mums, I feel that on the whole I did miss out on this front, by not having the opportunity to meet potential new mum friends for that much-needed support.

Therefore, going into childbirth for the first time, my birth plan went a bit like this: I'll have contractions, do my yoga breathing until the pain is too much to bear and I'll then have an epidural and have a baby. The End.

My tiny human had other ideas. She came six weeks early, which involved a couple of stints in hospital pre-birth, three days of being induced, a failed epidural, blind shit-the-bed panic and a drug-free-but-not-by-choice birth that had me climbing out of my skin and telling my husband never to ask me to do that EVER again.

Fast forward eighteen months and I was back a-bloody-gain with my second baby. And again six weeks early, following a couple of stints in hospital. This time, though, it involved a successful epidural and a textbook birth with me telling my hubby straight after that 'I would do that again tomorrow!'. Unbelievable, that two birth experiences could be so very different.

And I guess that's the point: we can only prepare for what is about to happen as best we can. That means doing whatever the hell you need to do to get yourself through it and bring your tiny human into the world as safely as possible. Whether this means meditating with Himalayan goats pre-birth, necking all the drugs available, reading every birthing book and technique going, exercising throughout to be as strong and as fit as possible – whatever it is, don't worry about what other people think of your techniques, ideas and values on the matter. Do what you need to do to get prepared.

They say that nothing can really prepare you for the reality of childbirth. However, I believe that talking about our experiences without fear of judgement, and being honest about its realities helps us to get as prepared as possible both physically and mentally.

Most importantly, what ever happens, when you come out the other side of it, please remember this: no matter what type of birth you have, no matter how you bring your tiny human into this world, you bloody rock and are truly magnificent!

DEAR FANNY– A LETTER TO MY PRE-BABY VAGINA

Now before we get cracking with sharing our birth stories, there is someone we need to invite to the party. After all, she plays a key role in getting our tiny humans here as safe and sound as possible. Oh yes, our dear friend Fanny.

Dearest Fanny,

Firstly, may I say that I have the upmost respect for the services you've rendered so far over the past thirty-nine years. I want to commend you on how reliable, trustworthy and downright supportive you've been of me and whatever strange friends, creams, waxing trends you've been subjected to – by me.

That's why I can't let you go into this next part of our journey without a bit of a heads-up about what's about to be coming your way.

I don't know quite how to break this to you, but in just a matter of weeks a tiny human will be making its way into this world via your good self!

Yes. Yes, I know, I get it. WTF, right? I hear ya, sista! I also can't get my head (or it seems my vagina) around the idea that a tiny human will soon be exiting us.

But as eye-watering, leg-crossing and palpitation-inducing the very idea of it is, similar to that dodgy Brazilian (no, I'm not referring to Bruno), we need to face this challenge head on (literally).

You see, as much as the midwife, the doctors and the hubby will be there to help us through, the rest of bringing this tiny human into the world safely – the most important part, in fact – is up to us: Team Vagina.

Therefore, in exchange for you keeping up your end of the bargain, I will make a couple of promises to you. I promise to do my best to keep you as informed as possible about what's happening (though I'm guessing that because you will have a front-row seat you will be more in the know than me!).

I promise to be as brave as I can be without being too proud or ashamed to ask for help if or when the pain gets too much to bear.

I promise to work with you as much as I can to get this baby here as safely and as quickly as humanly possible (the sooner it's over for both of us, the better).

I apologise now for any 'work' you may need post-baby.

However, to make up for this work, I promise that after the arrival of the tiny human I will have ice packs, a rubber ring, perineum cream and a cocktail of painkillers at the ready.

Most importantly, I do so solemnly declare — for the sake of us both — that I will not rush you into getting back to business as usual. I will give you time to recover and the R-E-S-P-E-C-T you deserve for being such a Vagina Rock Star!

Yours forever grateful and in awe of the wonderful work you do,

Me, the lady upstairs

MY FIRST BIRTH EXPERIENCE – 'NEVER ask me to do THAT again... EVER!'

Childbirth happens, I've discovered, when you're busy making birth plans.

I had a feeling my first baby was going to come early. I remember getting to seven months pregnant and looking at myself in the mirror clad in big pants and an unwired maternity bra (I know, what a vision, right?) and proclaiming to my husband: 'Jesus, I don't think I can get much bigger.' He laughed as only a man that has not been stretched beyond recognition can, and told me that I still had a long way to go yet (cheers, love!). However, that's not really what I meant. I wasn't on about the size of my tummy, so much as trying to describe how I felt. My tummy was heavy and low, I was feeling stretched as far as I could possibly stretch and, without sounding like a weirdo, my body just felt like it was getting ready to give birth.

Luckily a few days after this stretching epiphany, I was at the gynaecologist for my thirty-two-week checkup, which involved not only looking at the baby but also checking out my cervix too. From how I was feeling in my body, I just knew that he was going to tell me that something was up.

'Have you been having contractions?' came the voice from between my stirruped legs.

'Hmm, well, I don't know, as I don't know what they feel like [obvs!].'

'Well, have you been having any pains?'

'Now you mention it, for the past week I've been waking up in the middle of night in pain, like there is an earthquake going off in my tummy and it wakes me up.' (Oh, Jeez, Liv, I wonder what those could have been?)

'OK, well you've been having contractions and I know this because your cervix has shortened. It is a lot shorter than it should be at this stage. It may calm down and stay where it is and be OK. However, we need to monitor it and you need to start taking it easy.'

Shit.

I felt scared but also freaked out that I'd been so spot-on about my own body and how I was feeling. He told me that I could still work, but that I would have to work from home. Driving the long distance to work every day would bring on more contractions. So I agreed to stay put and set about working from home and taking it easy.

A week later, sat in the kitchen working from home (as promised), I was taken over by an overwhelming wave of pain. It took my breath away and filled me with a cold and prickly fear. A fear of realisation that this pain meant something. Jamie was in the lounge next door and I sat in the kitchen letting these waves of pain wash over me, whilst I took deep heavy breaths, not daring to voice my fears in case it made them real. I stayed exactly where I was, silent and thinking through the excruciating waves of pain for about five minutes. When my mind started screaming to me: 'You need to get to hospital', I called Jamie into the kitchen.

'We need to go to hospital,' I said calm as anything.

'What, what, what do you mean, what's wrong? Are you OK?'

'No, I'm in a lot of pain and have been for about five minutes.'

'Oh my God. Do you think they are labour pains? How painful are they?'

'Hmm, well I can't stand up.'

'Shit, right, I'll get the bags and the car.'

It was the middle of December in the Alps, and it was snowing (of course!). We lived up a mountain. The hospital was down the mountain and along lots of windy mountain roads. None of these facts were lost on me as I sat in our kitchen, unable to stand due to the pain I was in and watching the snow fall thick and fast outside. By the time Jamie had managed to get me into the car, I was doubled over in pain and panic was setting in. The baby was only thirty-three weeks, I could not give birth to a premature baby at the side of the road in the snow.

Driving in a full-blown snowstorm, Jamie was trying his hardest to calm me down whilst also trying to time the contractions. We hadn't got a clue what we were doing; we just knew we had to get to the hospital as soon as possible.

So there we were, the two of us and bump, me unable to speak properly through the pain and Jamie ashen-faced trying to navigate the winding roads, windscreen wipers going ten to the dozen as we were bombarded with big fat snowflakes. Every instinct in our bodies was telling us to get to the hospital as quickly as possible but then we remembered we had to drive slowly so as not to go skidding off the mountain roads. It was terrifying. All the way down, I was speaking to our baby, telling them to hold on, to stay put, to keep calm, it was not time yet for them to come.

The drive from hell finally came to an end. The attendants took one look at me half waddling, half bent in pain and trying to walk into the hospital reception, and they rushed me up to the maternity unit. The monitor confirmed that I was having strong contractions, so they explained to me that they would do all they could to calm them down and keep the baby put. The baby was checked over and we were told all was fine, and I was hooked up to a contraction machine for the rest of the night and given anti-contraction pills. The doctor also told me I was going nowhere (fine by me).

The contractions eventually died down, and after a night of monitoring, I was told that my cervix had shortened further and that I was going to have to have a steroid injection to help the baby's lungs develop in case the baby arrived prematurely (every sign was indicating as much). With the injection done and the contractions gone, I was allowed home but put on strict bed rest. The doctor warned me not too walk far (I was allowed to walk from my bed to the toilet and back, but that was it), I couldn't lift anything, I had to stop work immediately and I wasn't allowed to drive or go in the car for long distances. Effectively I was under house arrest, ordered to rest until the baby arrived. God, I wish I had appreciated this time more and let myself relax. Don't get me wrong, I was strictly feet up and bum on sofa, but my mind was racing all over the place, thinking of all the things I should be doing, watching my hubby take receipt of all the things I'd excitedly ordered for the nursery but which now I could not help set up, and feeling – what was that I was feeling? A little bit restless like I should be doing more and, dare I say, a little bit guilty because I couldn't. Oh yes, you never forget your first taste of mummy guilt – and I wasn't even officially a mummy yet!

I managed two weeks of sitting still and struggling to relax, worried about the baby constantly, knowing every day counted when it came to a baby coming prematurely. My nephew had been born earlier the same year at thirty-two weeks, so we had some first-hand experience of the challenges facing these little early birds and knew that the more days I could get under my belt the better. I managed a total of twelve extra days.

The contractions and tightening had continued and was pretty constant but nowhere near as uncomfortable or painful as the previous episode. However, I felt as though I was losing a small amount of water. Calling the hospital, we were told to come in. They examined me and the baby and said all was fine with the baby and that my cervix wasn't that much shorter than twelve days earlier, but they would check if I was losing amniotic fluid.

Me and the hubby will never forget the moment when the nurse confirmed that yes, I was losing amniotic fluid and that our baby would be with us within three days' time. We both stared up at the midwife with the goofiest of grins, overwhelmed with relief that the baby was OK to be born at this time, and ridiculously excited that we were going to be real-life parents, that the two of us were going to become the three of us in just a matter of days. This was it. It was happening!

We had been reassured that our baby was healthy, and not in any danger: the steroid injection and the fact that I'd managed to keep the baby put for an extra couple of weeks meant that the baby was fine to be delivered at thirty-four weeks. They told us that we had a maximum window of three days to give birth, as my waters had started to break. Otherwise, they would have to give me a C-section – on Christmas Day. Oh yes, our end-of-January baby was now a festive baby; it seemed like the turkey might not be the only thing getting sliced and diced on Christmas day.

Over the course of the next three days, I was induced three times, each day bringing a new midwife and a different method each time. I endured the joys of an overzealous sweep, a pessary and a drip – and I have to say that it was the pessary which left me in the most discomfort. On Christmas Eve, I was told I was finally dilated and that they were moving me up to the labour ward so that we were closer to everything we needed to be close to (namely the epidural, ha ha). Looking back now, I am really proud and a bit in awe of how calm I was. I really did take it all in my stride and felt ready to go into childbirth. I was doing my yoga breathing through the pain and felt in control. This feeling of being in control helped me mentally, and made me feel prepared for what lay ahead.

The nurses all knew that my plan was to carry on dealing with the contractions this way, for as long as I could, and that then I would have an epidural. Things were all going swimmingly until I was asked if I was ready to go into the labour room since I was in active labour. Idiot here decided instead, to opt for another quick walk around the ward before we headed in for my epidural. As Julia Roberts said to the snooty shop assistant in *Pretty Woman*, 'Big mistake. Huge!'

That decision to take an extra stroll meant that I missed my window of opportunity for the birth I had planned. The birth for which I was mentally prepared. When I was first asked to go to the labour room, the anaesthetist was available and ready. By the time I was ready to go into the room, she had been called to attend to an emergency case, and I would have to wait. Wait? Oh my days, telling a woman in active labour to wait when all she wants is a goddam epidural takes a very brave soul. My hubby was the one who had to break it to me. Through gritted teeth, I told him in my best demonic and savage voice that I wasn't being rude, '. . . but please stop talking to me. Don't talk to me, don't touch me. Just leave me be to get through this and wait.' I proceeded to pace around like a caged and angry tiger in a small circle, counting up to ten, on and on and on, around and around and around. I was consumed with such a savage and desperate pain that I no longer wanted to be in my own body. Instead I wanted to disown it and run as fast as I could away from the burning and disgusting pain and come back when it was all over. Oh dear Lord, why did I go for that damn walk and where was the damn anaesthetist?

She finally turned up, and I was so twisted in agony and despair at the level of pain I was in that I felt betrayed by my own body. I was desperate for the epidural – but despite wanting nothing more than those drugs, I've got to admit that actually having the epidural terrified me. I'd heard that if I moved whilst they were doing it, I could be paralysed forever. Not a great thought to have when they're trying to get a needle in your spine during the ever-decreasing windows of time between body-shaking contractions that rendered it impossible to do anything, let alone keep still. My calm was starting to unravel, replaced with unadulterated fear and me repeating to myself: 'This is not what I had planned.'

My epidural made me feel sick to my stomach because it took a good few attempts until she was able to do it safely. Once it was done, though, I told myself that I could relax and just start to get my head in gear for the delivery. My mind had been filled with nothing but unrelenting pain up to this point. I just needed a window of respite to get myself together – which the epidural gave me. It was pure bliss, like an ice cube on a hot day, or a warm bath after a long run. I fell into the most blissful of sleeps and slept deeply for a full hour. When I woke up, my hubby calmly told me they were going to come and break my waters when I was ready and that we would then start with the delivery. I was ready. The epidural, the loss of pain and the sleep had renewed and restored my confidence. I was ready. 'Back in control.'

Just as these words left my mouth, a wave of excruciating pain crashed down onto me, breaking my hopes and resolve against its angry shoreline and leaving me face down in the water, unable to catch my breath before the next, more powerful wave of unspeakable pain came crashing down on me. What the hell was going on? My brain grasped for answers and air. I was hooked up to the epidural and should have been able to self-administer it depending on my level of pain, but no matter how many times I hit that button, nothing was happening.

I was now surrounded by a machine with its alarms going off, in even more pain than before and with nowhere to run, nowhere to hide. The anaesthetist was called back in, along with numerous midwives who couldn't work out what was wrong with the machine; they rushed and fussed around me, checking wires whilst I was almost levitating off the bed in agony. One moment I'd been having the best sleep of my life, all warm, calm and safe, and the next I was trapped in the jaws of hell with no way out and no one to rescue me.

The midwives were all talking to me in French. My poor mind was now understanding only my body's fear and pain and it could not decipher a word they were saying, so I started to block them all out. My husband managed to break through the barrier of pain I was trapped behind and translate, telling me that there was nothing they could do, the machine had stopped working and that it was too late to try and give me a second epidural because the baby was coming. The look on his face must have mirrored my own horror; I have never seen him look like that at me before or since, telling me that I was on my own, that I had to somehow get through what was about to happen and there was nothing he or anybody else could do.

I grabbed his hand, looked him dead in the eye and told him to just tell me what I needed to do and I would do it . . . I then remember telling him never to ask me to do this again. I screamed, 'Promise me!'. He did and then, with him on one side and a midwife on the other, I grabbed their hands and stepped off the precipice, into the flames.

The rest of the birth is one giant blur of pain, indescribable noises and shocking realities that shook me to my very core and left me broken mentally and physically. I may have been physically strong enough to get through childbirth, but my mind was not equipped to deal with the level of panic, pain and shock that I experienced during it.

Through the whole experience, there was a moment of numb peace: the moment I met Éva. When she was placed on me – a hot, gooey comfort with wild, searching eyes and a perfection like no other – I knew her instantly. And boy, did she show us who she was from the moment she was born. Six weeks early, as strong as an ox and weighing an incredibly healthy premature weight of 5.2 pounds. The doctors were surprised, and pleased to tell us that she was fine and healthy, and that she didn't need to go in the incubator they had ready for her. She even breastfed straightaway. She was an incredible little powerhouse, as dainty as a baby bird but as strong and as sure-footed as a Trojan.

It's both funny and reassuring to think back to the sureness of the connection I felt with Éva, this little being I had never even met. From the moment I became pregnant with her, I felt this overwhelming bond with her, and when she was born and I finally got to meet this little girl I'd been dreaming about for the past several months, the bond became even stronger. I knew beyond anything else I'd ever known that we belonged together and that I would take the best care of her. To say I loved her would not even come close to my feelings for her. We were one: she was me and I was her and that was that.

Now, unfortunately, this is where we say goodbye to the old me, the mum that you have gotten to know between these pages, via these confessions and the stories so far. Her time is coming to an end. She's still around in some form, but to the person she was before this moment we now need to bid farewell.

You see, in the labour room that night I gained a beautiful, feisty, strong-hearted little girl, but I lost something too. I left that labour room with a baby in my arms, but I also lost a piece of myself, a piece that I have never been able to get back.

We had no idea at the time what awaited us on the other side of those labour room doors. A life as a family, yes, but also waiting was one of the fiercest and most challenging battles I'd ever had to face.

We spent two hours in the delivery room with Éva. She was nestled on my chest, feeding and getting cuddles whilst I watched and adored her through a screen of bewildered calm. Something had shifted in the universe because our little daughter was now a part of it. However, something had also shifted in me, and it would take a good several months before we realised the size of this seismic shift and the devastating repercussions it would have on the little family that had been forged together in that delivery room, that night.

THE EVERY MUM GUIDE TO CHILDBIRTH

We have all been there, fit to bursting, rubbing our fast-expanding tummy and hanging off every last detail from a mum painting the story of her birth in full technicolour glory. I've been there, listening away whilst pregnant with my first, hoping that the kind of story I would get to tell would be closer to the nice and positive experiences I was hearing rather than the ones where I sat open-mouthed and cross-legged listening to the poor mum who had to go through such an ordeal. As fate would have it, two babies have given me experience of both: a birth that left me traumatised and suffering from postnatal depression and a birth that was so textbook and straightforward that I told my husband I would definitely have another baby. Go figure!

That's the thing with childbirth I wish I had been more aware of the first time around. No two births are the same, no two experiences will leave you feeling the same as the other. Yes, it can be an amazing experience –and yes, it can also take you to the depths of despair. So, when preparing for the battle that is bringing your tiny human into the world, isn't it about time that we prepared ourselves both physically and mentally by being open about all the different types of experiences, open and without judgement? By throwing away our expectations and 'perfect birth' plans, and easing off the pressure we place on ourselves to have the perfect birth, the one that goes exactly according to plan. And start believing that a birth which keeps the mother and baby as healthy and safe as possible is the only type of birth to focus on – regardless of how it happens.

With that in mind, here is my Every Mum Guide to Childbirth, including all the things I wish I had known before I entered the labour room.

• *It will eventually be over!*

'Thank God,' I hear you all cry! Yes, regardless of what type of birth you choose or is chosen for you due to bad luck, bad timing and circumstance, it does have an ending. That may be hard to believe when you're going through it, but that baby is coming out one way or another. The process of bringing your tiny human into the world will not go on forever! Whether you are having the birth from hell or the birth from heaven, it will eventually come to an end. Amen to that!

• *You may not have the birth you want*

Not the news any of us mums to be want to hear – but why the hell do we sugarcoat the fact that the birth we have been planning may not happen? Like all things in motherhood, by managing our expectations and the pressures we place on ourselves to deliver our perfect birth experience, we are also decreasing our chances of feeling like a failure if things don't go according to plan. Childbirth is a tricky bloody matter involving lots of different variables outside of our control. Therefore, we need to go into it fully aware that things don't always go according to plan and instead to prepare ourselves (mentally) for the possibility that they won't.

• *You may have an amazing birth*

The concept of an 'amazing' childbirth experience was completely alien to me after the traumatic birth of my first child. I stared in wonder at mums who told me they had 'enjoyed' childbirth and that it had been a 'wonderful' experience – surely their drugs should have worn off by now? Apparently not; they really had enjoyed it: the birth of my second was the opposite to my first. I thought it was an amazing experience and felt elated following it. So, for any mum out there who has also experienced a traumatic birth: as unbelievable as it may sound to you right now, I promise you that a good birth is possible.

• *It's OK to ask for help post-baby*

A lot of mums feel traumatised after childbirth. Then, thanks to social pressures and the expectations we put on ourselves, we feel abnormal and like shit mums for feeling anything but elated at the thought of our baby, the birth and our new life in general. You are not alone. There is help out there to help you process your birth experience. Grab it with both hands as soon as you can, and punch that bastard that is post-birth guilt and trauma in the face! (For support with birth trauma please see the services listed on pages 236–238.)

• You are in control

Easy to say when you're not five centimetres dilated and climbing the wall in excruciating pain. So remember it is your baby, your body and your choice on how you want things to happen when it comes to pushing your tiny human out into the world. Whether that's a home birth, epidural, water birth or good old gas and air, the choice is yours. As long as you and the baby are healthy and in a good condition, then you reign supreme and those around you have to do as you wish.

• It's normal to have stitches!

Come on, let's get real! Our bodies are bloody amazing things, but even the hardiest of vaginas are in need of some patching up after pushing what feels like a tiny elephant through a walnut shell! Seriously! Yes, I too squirmed at the thought of this, thinking how awful it would be to have stitches in my nether regions. However, it is totally normal, it happens to most women, and it's nothing to be worried about – after what your vagina has already been through in childbirth, stitches will be a walk in the park.

• You may poo yourself!

I think I was dreading this more than the actual thought of childbirth when pregnant with my first! So much so that at six centimetres dilated and mid-contractions I made my hubby walk me to the loo because I couldn't imagine anything worse than pooing in front of strangers! What a bloody fool! Three centimetres and a failed epidural later, I wouldn't have cared if I had pebbledashed the whole bloody team of midwives! Needless to say that with my second I never even thought about it. Did I poo myself? Who the hell knows? And seriously, who the hell cares? I promise you will want to give a shit (literally) but you won't even know about it if it does happen.

• *Scream, grunt, swear*

Admit it, we've all been there watching *One Born Every Minute* whilst a mum screams and grunts her baby into existence and found ourselves thinking, 'I will never sound like that!' Pah! Ha, ha! Don't kid yourselves. Most importantly, do whatever it takes to get you through it. From screaming profanities to making sounds you never thought possible, these noises will help you get through whatever you need to get through, so just let it rip!

• *You are brave enough!*

Whatever happens to you through your birth experience, you need to know this: no matter how brave you think you are in normal everyday life, no matter how little faith you have in yourself, no matter how low you feel your pain threshold is and no matter if you are the biggest scaredy-cat of all time, you are brave enough and strong enough to bring your tiny human into the world.

• *Did I mention it will eventually be over?!*

Yes, like everything in life, it does have an ending. You will get there, and no matter how knackered, distraught, amazed, euphoric, and sore you are, you have brought a beautiful tiny human into this world. You are magnificent!

WHY NO MUM SHOULD BE JUDGED ON HOW SHE BRINGS HER TINY HUMAN INTO THE WORLD

One of the main things that can suck the enjoyment and our sense of achievement out of childbirth — alongside failed epidurals, tearing and eye-bulging pain, obvs — is the judgement we can feel post-baby when it comes to the question of how we brought our tiny human into the world. I for one, was floored by it. My response was to write the following article for my blog and *The Huffington Post*, which got such a fantastic response from mums across the world that I want to share it with you here:

What's the worst thing about childbirth?

Forget the pain, the stretching and the climb the wall, 'Shit, there's no turning back' fear. You then feel as though you have to face the gauntlet of being judged on the methods by which your child arrived. Did you opt for every drug going? Or did you instead bite down on a bit of bark, freshly plucked from the garden, whilst you squatted over a bucket, birthing au naturel.

SERIOUSLY, who cares?!

Apparently a hell of a lot of people! Don't they realise that it's none of their business whether you pushed your baby out through a teeny hole in your body or whether a surgeon had to slice a hole in your tummy to get your baby out? Why, oh why are people so bothered? And why do us mums feel like we are being scored or failed depending on our birthing methods and choices?

Does it make us lesser human beings if we choose to have pain relief to aide the safe arrival of our baby? And why do some women feel the need to proclaim on their Facebook status and to anyone who will listen that they did it the 'natural' way and did not 'give in' by opting for pain relief or a c-section. NEWSFLASH! Giving birth is not a competition and we are doing a dangerous disservice to every mum out there by turning it into one.

As mums we all have our own plans concerning how to achieve the best birth experience for ourselves. Mine was to get as far as I could with breathing techniques and then opt for a big fat epidural to get me through the rest. However, as all us procreators are aware, childbirth happens when you're busy making birth plans. An hour into my epidural, its magical, pain-eradicating powers ceased working and instead dumped me alone in the wilderness, grunting, screaming and willing for any form of warrior prowess to conjure itself up and get 'this baby out of me as fast as possible'. So did I have a 'natural' birth? I am not ashamed to admit that the pain, stretching and downright speed of it all felt anything but natural.

Do I feel smug or better than the next mum because I had to endure the unspeakable pain of pushing my baby out into the world drug free? Do I feel this makes me a better or stronger person compared to a woman who had an elected c-section? Hell no, the only thing I feel is royally cheated and hacked off that the epidural didn't work and that the birth I had planned was snatched out of my hands, leaving me in total shock and bewilderment.

Surely, getting your baby here in the safest way for both baby and mum is what should be the main concern when discussing childbirth? Surely, asking a mum how her birth experience was for her should be the only question? Instead of judging and scoring women on the types of birth they end up having, the main aim should be to ensure that every mum (despite the obvious physical pain they may experience) feels satisfied with their birth experience and that it hasn't traumatised them to the point where it is now affecting their new life as being a mum.

You see, that's the thing about opinions on childbirth. The negative effects of certain opinions can cause a serious domino effect in the life of a mum, leaving her traumatised if she didn't have the birth she had planned and hoped for and then feeling judged by those who feel she should have done it differently.

This mum and every mum like her needs to be given a break and a huge congratulatory pat on the back. Not only has she brought a new life into this world, but she has done it under circumstances she had not planned for, wanted or considered. It should be this woman who gets the accolades and who is held high on the birthing pedestals. The woman who despite wanting a home birth is instead rushed into A&E for an emergency c-section, the woman who despite planning pain relief ends up giving birth on the bathroom floor drug-free. The woman who after pushing for hours is whipped into surgery to have her most intimate of areas cut to allow her child to be unceremoniously dragged into the world and the woman who, regardless of outside opinion, sticks to her gut instincts in order to have the birth she wants. Therefore, every mum who grows and brings a new person into this world, regardless of the means we choose to do this or the unforeseen circumstances we are dealt, should be applauded not judged.

There is no failure to be found in any female brave enough to go through the process of childbirth, no matter what that process may be. There is no such thing as 'giving in' or taking the 'easy option' when it comes to childbirth. Instead, the heroic act of childbirth, no matter what shape or form it is delivered in, is one to be bowed down to with awe, respect and rewarded with the admiration it deserves.

CHAPTER 5

BECOMING MUM – THE EARLY DAYS

DEAR YOU – A LETTER TO THE NEW MUM

Dear You,

'You are doing so, so great!'
Yes, I'm talking about you.
YOU who hasn't slept for more than two hours straight in what feels like since the beginning of time.
YOU whose vagina is in such climb-the-wall-pain you can barely breathe without wanting to sell off your lady bits to the highest bidder.
YOU whose C-section scars are leaving you feeling helpless for not being able to pick up the baby, move around like normal and do everything you thought you would be doing as a new mum.
YOU, who are traumatised to your very core following your harrowing experiences of childbirth but feel too scared to talk about them.
YOU who are working your way through breast-feeding via cracked nipples, the pain urging you to give up but the mix of determination and guilt making you carry on regardless of your own health because you don't want to 'let down' your tiny human.
YOU who desperately wanted to breast-feed but couldn't and are now feeling like you've failed.

YOU who didn't want to breast-feed and now feel judged.

I'm talking to YOU, the mum who is taking everything in her stride.

YOU, the mum struggling to get out of the door before the next feed, nappy change or tiny human tantrum.

To YOU, the mum missing her old life and counting down the days until you can return to work.

To YOU, the mum for whom the very idea of returning to work is making you feel sick to the stomach.

To YOU, the mum attending another playdate, park visit, mother and baby group and feeling like you've got more of a social life now than ever before.

To YOU, the mum housebound due to crippling anxiety, postnatal depression and unable to see a way out.

To YOU, the mum wondering if you and your partner will survive the mayhem, exhaustion and financial and emotional strains becoming parents has put on your relationship.

To YOU, the mum feeling lonely and isolated.

To ALL of YOU mums doing the best you can to be the best mum you can be to your tiny human despite battling with some or all of the above.

YOU, my fellow mums are doing a fantastic job!

Love,
Liv xx

MY STORY: 'IT WAS THE BEST OF TIMES, IT WAS THE WORST OF TIMES . . .'

The night I gave birth to our beautiful little girl was the night things changed forever. Not just because her birth started us on the path of being a family but because (without us knowing) it also placed us on the path to living with a maternal mental health illness. A one-way path that led me to the destination where I recognized I had been changed forever.

I left the labour room with a baby in my arms but I also left behind there a piece of myself. A piece that made me who I was. Someone, with an unassuming optimism and the belief that staying positive was enough to ensure everything would be OK. I could get through anything.

The person I was when I entered that labour room, is no longer here. I now know that she is gone forever. Even though I am well and free of the illness, I will never get that person back. I will never be her again.

Now, I feel like I need to step in here for a mo, just in case you are worrying that I am getting a little bit too dark. Admittedly, things for me did get very dark for a while. However, this book and our friendship is built on being able to share our stories of motherhood in all their shades and all their glory. This honesty and commitment to facing things and addressing things head on (no matter how dark) is at the heart of what is going to empower me, you and every mum reading these words to make their mental health a priority. This is going to act as a much needed and vital reminder that every mum deserves the right to enjoy motherhood. And that some of our most challenging of times lead us to become the most formidable of people.

So let's go through the darkness together . . .

Back on the labour ward, this feeling of leaving something, a part of me, behind that night explains (now) why I felt so desolate in the days following her birth. I was a shell of my former self. Yes, exhausted and in pain from the birth, but more than that, there was just something missing. Despite having the one thing that was supposed to complete me, I was somehow more incomplete than I ever had been before.

Looking back now, I can see that just hours after giving birth, huge pieces of me had already gone AWOL. The cornerstone of my personality, my self-confidence, had started to erode. The rot had set in. My body and mind, exhausted from childbirth, had nothing left in

70

reserve to provide a defence against such a silent and swift attack. An attack that was now running amok through my happiness, undermining my ability to feel joy and my strength to cope with whatever life throws at me.

My illness (of which I was unaware of at the time) savaged my very soul. It took my self-identity, and allowed feelings of fear, anger, anxiety and isolation to puff out their chests and flood into every vacant corner of my being.

This sense of desolation, of feeling that I had been taken over and no longer existed, was there from the moment I was wheeled out of that labour room. Surely, though, I just needed some rest? Just needed to get myself together and get on with being mum and then everything would go back to normal and I'd be OK, wouldn't I?

THE EARLY WARNING SIGNS THAT SOMETHING WASN'T RIGHT

• Birth Trauma

My first cry for help, which should have triggered the first alarm bell, was when a midwife came to see me in hospital a day or so after the birth and asked, 'How was the birth for you?'.

We were still in neonatal being monitored and the midwife came in to see me. Sat down on my bed with my hubby watching us both and spoke these words which quite simply broke my heart and struck something so raw in me that it literally sucked the breath right out of me.

I sobbed – big, ugly, heart-wrenching sobs – as I repeated my answer to her. The only answer that could ever exist for me in response to such a question: 'Shocking . . . Shocking . . . Shocking.' Painfully spoken in between my guttural and impossible-to-contain sobs of despair.

This was my first 'moment' of truth, the first indication that something was not quite right.

However, for reasons I still don't know or understand, this cry went unanswered, unacknowledged and unmonitored. Perhaps it was because I was a new mum who had only just given birth to a premature baby, so the midwife thought me having a good cry was only 'natural'. Or perhaps the midwife didn't feel my response was enough to put me on their radar or to probe deeper into my feelings of despair? I still do not have the answers. I still question even now, Why didn't I realise this was not the 'normal' way to feel? Why did my internal alarm bell not go off? Why did neither my husband nor I realise something was not quite right?

I often wonder how different the outcome would have been if the midwife and doctors had understood that things were not as they should be or if I had realised I was ill. It was only months later after being diagnosed with postnatal depression (PND) and being able to talk to friends about what I had been through, that I shared this story with a close friend who had given birth around the same time. When her midwife had asked her the very same question about her birth experience, she replied that she had a really good experience and that she felt well and happy about the birth and her recovery from it. Surely my response was not the response of a happy and relieved mum. Surely this was not the 'normal' response? So why was this not noticed? My experiences afterward would have been monumentally different if it had been.

Now I know that if I had been aware of the effects that a negative birth experience can have on your state of mind, if I had been aware that 'birth trauma' was a thing that could actually happen. It would have been on my radar and also my husband's. I would have recognised it. I would have been mentally prepared for the possibility of it. And I would have asked for help. Oh yes, the cruel beauty of hindsight.

• Crippling anxiety and panic attacks

During those early days in hospital, another guest to my post-birth party was a new and soon to become not so welcome friend: crippling anxiety. And in much the same way that many of the symptoms manifested themselves, it was sort of always present from the moment I became a mum. In fact, it jumped into the spotlight and made its debut in my life whilst I was still in hospital with Éva.

Éva was due to have her first bath, something I had said my hubby should do, so he could have his very own 'first experience' with her. (I thought he should do the baby's first bath as I got to do all the other firsts.)

We'd been told the time to take her and we were on our way to the neonatal unit, Éva being wheeled in her plastic cot by Daddy and me shuffling in agony and tracksuit bottoms behind, when it hit me. The only way I can describe it is to say that it was like the whole world tilted on its axis and then came crashing down on me. It knocked the life and breath out of me and made me feel like I was falling down a black hole. I think I started to pass out; it was only the terror of falling into my daughter's cot and sending her crashing to the concrete hospital floor that enabled me to hold onto the edge of reality and fight the urge to fall into the all–consuming and welcome darkness.

This would be the first of many severe and debilitating panic attacks I endured over the next three years. The very strength of them left me feeling listless, disorientated and exhausted. Yet at the time, despite nearly passing out with panic as I wheeled my daughter to what should have been a happy experience, her first bath, no warning bells rang, no alarms were triggered. We were three days into parenthood, exhausted, bewildered and believing this was just all part of the course. How bloody lost were we?!

The panic attacks continued sporadically once we left hospital, but the panic was constant, leaving me just teetering on the edge of control. There was no off switch. I remember once describing to my husband how I felt as though all the atoms in my body were shaking violently and consistently underneath the surface of my skin. That I could almost hear them clattering and crashing up against each other, sending violent ripples along the surface. Sometimes I would expect to look down at my arms and see my skin rippling like ferocious waves crashing against the shoreline of my wrist. It made me feel weirdly exhilarated, moving around at warp speed, and utterly exhausted – all at the same time. It gave me the running-on-empty energy to blitz the house, sterilise all the surfaces and bottles, do all the washing, rearrange her clothes drawers and do a workout all whilst she napped. However, this supercharged efficiency never allowed me the time to eat or rest – the two most important things I should have been doing as a new mum whilst my tiny human slept.

In fact, come to think of it now, I never sat down. Ever. I did everything standing up, completing different jobs that had to be ticked off my never-ending To Do list. I rushed around manically to complete all my chores whilst she slept, fuelled by my belief that if I didn't complete everything I would have failed at being a good mum. I never sat down. I never rested. I never questioned my behaviour. This was my life.

This was every mum's life, wasn't it?

• *Not wanting visitors*

One of the strangest things – one of the biggest signs that something was wrong – was that following the birth of Éva and even whilst we were still in hospital I didn't want any visitors. I call this 'strange' because everyone else I know who's had a baby could not wait to show them off to the world and have their family and friends meet them as soon as possible. But after having Éva I just did not want anyone to visit us. This wasn't something I ever admitted or voiced out loud. I just engineered it so that it didn't happen.

My family were all back in the UK and already had flights booked for a couple of weeks before her actual due date. As Éva arrived six weeks early, this meant that it worked out that we had around two weeks after she was born until they were due to see us. They asked if they could come out straightaway, but I managed to somehow fob them off by saying that we were still in hospital and that it would be more helpful if they waited and were there with us when we were out of hospital. That worked.

Friends who lived locally tried their hardest to visit, but having a premature baby made it easy to discourage them – due to feed times, tests, me being tired, etc.

A good friend of mine (who'd also had her little girl six weeks premature, just a few weeks before me) was desperate to come and visit us. She wanted to meet Éva and make sure I was OK. However, all she got from me was total radio silence or excuses from me via my hubby. Several months later she admitted to me that she found my reluctance to have visitors a bit odd and then became increasingly worried about it, thinking that something wasn't quite right. I then admitted to her that she had been right and that it was a sign of how ill I was that I didn't want to see anyone.

At the time, I didn't know why I didn't want to see people. All I knew was that the anxiety residing in the pit of my stomach was so strong that I had to do whatever I could to get out of having visitors – and that I was so ashamed to be feeling this way, I never voiced these fears to anyone.

Whilst we were in hospital, I had a grand total of three visitors over the two weeks we were there. This all now feels desperately sad, and all I want to do is go back to that hospital and give myself a huge hug, to call my mum and my forceful friend and beg them to come and see me, beg them not to listen to my excuses but just to barge their way into my hospital room and give me the reassurance and support I didn't know I needed but for which I was so desperate.

During these early days, I was in such a mess – in retrospect, the most shocking realisation is that it happened so suddenly and so completely that I had no time to prepare for it. There was no slow burn, no gradual build-up. I had my baby, I spent two hours with her in the labour room following her birth, I left the room and was wheeled back to my bed (whilst my hubby took Éva for a few more routine tests) and then I was given some food and told to sleep. I ate. I closed my eyes. I went to sleep. I woke up and the illness was there and I was powerless to recognise it – and therefore, unable to do anything about it, before it was too late.

Writing about these early days has made me feel quite sick to my stomach. Remembering that desperate and anxiety-riddled state makes me feel – even now, four years on – as though I could physically throw up, just to eject the memories. As I am writing this at home, alone, I am crying. Crying with sorrow for the absolute wretchedness this new mum went through, all on her own, trapped inside her own mind, a mind that had turned against her. It has the well and recovered me asking: Hadn't she got enough on her plate? Why could she have not been left alone to enjoy motherhood the way she had envisioned? Why had no one warned her? Why was she left to enter motherhood without the knowledge that becoming a mum can affect your mental health? Why did she not know that there was such a thing as maternal mental health?

My heart aches with sorrow when I remember that new mum, sitting in hospital with her new premature baby, in crippling pain, trying to keep a grip on her own sanity and wondering why she was not feeling as ecstatically happy and content as she always felt she would feel after becoming a mum. Waiting hour after hour for something to click into place, for the cogs of her emotions to start to turn so she could stop feeling so empty, so desolate and so alone and isolated. Stop feeling so numb, and start feeling something. Anything.

The mind is a silent and cruel, cruel bully. Unless we are armed with the correct knowledge, we will not be properly equipped to stand up to it. So when I look back on that mum and her guarded smiles, I see someone caught in a trap, having chunks of herself being unceremoniously torn away. No one can see what is taking place. No one is privy to her suffering – not even her closest of family, despite being right next to her whilst the attacks are taking place. She herself cannot scream for help; she is bound and gagged by perceptions – her own and society's – of how she should be coping. She sits there, smiling whilst watching pieces of herself, pieces that she treasures the most and which make her who she is, being stripped away and set alight. And she has no idea if she will ever have them or anything close to them again.

All this. All this during the happiest time of her life. How bloody cruel and unjust is this illness?

IF THIS IS YOU

If you are currently this mum, please know that you are not alone and that you have done nothing wrong. You do not deserve to be going through what you are going through. You do deserve to be well again. You do deserve to be experiencing the motherhood you had dreamt about. You do deserve the right to enjoy motherhood and there is support out there to help you reclaim this right – *see* pages 236–238.

GOING HOME WITH A BABY AND PND

The first two weeks at home after being discharged from hospital are now (as they are for pretty much any new mum) a bit of a blur – a mix of sleepless nights, feed schedules, trying to breast-feed and crippling pain as I tried to recover from the birth.

It's fair to say that those first moments at home didn't quite live up to my expectations. Pre-baby I thought that being back at home would be filled with visiting friends, showing her off to the world and taking lots of walks with her in the brand new and swanky buggy. However, due to the amount of pain (thanks to the stitches), I could literally only walk to the toilet and back before I was wincing in agony. So I spent the first part of being at home literally cocooned with just Éva and me. Home was where I felt safest, just the two of us, fathoming out our routine and each other. Just being us. This is when the illness really started to take hold, and what should have been the warning signs of the illness became the norm. Instead of standing out like a sore thumb against the backdrop of my new mum life, they were part of everyday life.

• *Feeling overprotective*

My parents came to visit two weeks in – and as only parents can they picked up on a couple of things. These, if they had been probed further or viewed more continuously, would have highlighted that things were a little off. Now, I don't know if my parents can even remember either of these two moments; to the outside world they were so small and insignificant, but to me it felt as though someone was scraping their finger over an open, raw wound.

The first moment involved my mum. It was the first time she had met Éva and, like any new grandparent meeting her new grandchild, she wanted to give her a cuddle and hold her. It was the first time I'd realised how difficult it was for me to hand her over to someone else (even my own mum). Watching someone else hold her, be responsible for her, sent my anxiety levels into overdrive and made me feel sick to my stomach. I remember the moment so well, me sitting on the sofa, Éva (safely) in my arms and my mum (the woman I trust most in the world) sitting opposite me, looking at me expectantly, with the unspoken request in the air of 'Please can I hold her?'. I felt frozen, could feel the warm and reassuring weight of Éva in my arms and was unable to move. The rational side of my brain which was still functioning (if only on a part-time basis) was trying to get the message to my arms to pass her over, but I just couldn't summon them to move. It was probably only a moment that lasted no more than a minute, but it seemed to go on for an eternity as I battled with myself internally.

It took my mum to say the words 'Do you not want me to hold

her?' to snap me (and my disabled arms) into action and hand her over whilst the desperate person inside me screamed:

'NO! No, I don't want you or anyone else to hold her and I don't know why. But just hand her back to me right now before something awful happens to her.'

I went through this, to varying degrees of hell, during every visit we had and every social gathering I attended. Everyone (naturally) wanted to give her a cuddle while I was desperately going out of my mind and dreading every request, until I could stand no more and would do anything I could to escape the situation. Often I found myself so heartbroken about having to hand her over that I would have to leave the room just to be able to endure it.

• Scared to let the world in

My dad was the one who touched upon another elephant in the room when he turned up one day to the house and asked me why the lounge curtains were still drawn? It was nearing lunchtime and a beautiful crisp and sunny winter's day. This simple question sent me reeling in panic. I felt as though I was on the verge of being found out – though for what I couldn't quite figure out. I remember feeling that with this simple question my dad was unlocking the door to an ugly part of me and revealing it for all to see.

At the time, these feelings confused me, but they were so unnerving that I felt I had to cover myself and fix the mask that had slipped. I remember replying as nonchalantly as possible that I didn't even realise they were still shut – silly and tired mummy that I was – and went and opened them whilst rolling my eyes at myself.

Little did my mum and dad know that those two simple and unassuming questions hit at the heart of the illness that was growing stronger every day, and trying to stake a claim over me.

I was scared of anyone else holding her and I was becoming increasingly scared to leave the house and let the outside world in. Keeping the curtains closed and shut was keeping the world out, keeping the dangers out and my new family safe. Trying to open those curtains that day and handing Éva over to others to hold went against everything that my body was telling me to do.

I know they would never want me to feel I had to apologise to them for any of this. However, I am sorry, Mum and Dad, for not having the words to tell you what I was going through. I'm sorry that I didn't share my illness and my depths of despair with you. I'm sorry for shutting you out and for putting on a show for you that everything was OK, when it wasn't. But please take solace in the fact that you two were the ones who instinctively picked up on two of my biggest fears back in those first weeks. I know deep down that if I hadn't been living in a different country to you, that if you had been seeing me more regularly, you would have eventually figured out and voiced that something was not right with me.

• Dealing with visitors

As we were living abroad, the visiting period from UK family and friends was intense. Expectations for me to be a social butterfly were high, everyone pushing to spend as much time with my new tiny human as possible – dropping in unannounced, asking to babysit overnight and commenting how little they had held her or suggesting that I was being 'unsociable' for wanting some downtime with just me and my new baby.

Looking back, it was one of the most horrendous times. My undiagnosed illness was chipping away at my confidence, leaving me unable to stand up for myself or to put my needs first and say when enough had become enough. Too much.

Needless to say, I breathed an almighty sigh of relief when they were finally over. As difficult as these few weeks were, they also taught me some invaluable lessons – which eventually made me resolute about how I would do things differently if we were lucky enough to have a second baby, and which have made me passionate in my belief of how new mums should be treated.

As a new mum in the early throes of motherhood, we should not be put under any additional pressure to be a certain way, to attend a social gathering or to pass our new babies around as much as possible, if we don't want to do so. Those early weeks are some of the most precious and most vulnerable for every new mum, and all mums (whether ill or not) need unconditional support, care and space to figure out their new roles and lives – no judgement.

Some mums don't have the energy or confidence to voice when enough is enough. So it's up to the rest of us to be sympathetic and supportive and to treat them with the respect they deserve for the amazing act of growing and bringing a tiny life into this world. No one knows the complexity of emotions running through the mind of a new mum. No one knows what she may be battling internally or feeling overwhelmed by. We all need to remember that every new mum is a goddess in her own right, she is the queen of her little universe and deserves nothing but our love, admiration and support.

• Leaving the house

Leaving the house during these first few weeks at home was physically impossible. I remember thinking I needed to pull myself together and stop being such a wimp, and just get myself and our new family out of the house for our first walk. So on one sunny morning, I decided we were going to take her for her first walk – and it was going to be amazing. I made it twenty metres down the road, grimacing in agony with every shuffle, holding onto the buggy for support. Then my hubby took one look at me and asked if I was OK; I'd started turning green. I admitted through bitter tears that I thought I was going to pass out. As much as I wanted to, I could not take another step. We turned ourselves around and returned home, me feeling like a terrible mum because I'd failed at what should have been one of the easiest and most fun things to do as a new mum – to take my daughter on her first walk.

I tried to reassure myself that, once I'd recovered physically, everything would be OK and I'd go walking with her every day. What I didn't foresee was that once the physical pain barrier had been lifted and I could walk without wincing, the mental barrier on most days would render me incapable of leaving the house for fear of something awful happening to her. There were days that I couldn't scale that mental barrier, but on the days when I did finally make it out of the house I would be racked with such anxiety that every nerve ending in my body was on high alert to the slightest noise or movement that might cause potential danger and the death of my precious baby girl.

Now, we were living in a mountain resort in the French Alps at the height of winter, so as you can imagine, navigating steep icy paths sent my fear and anxiety into overdrive: my knuckles were white as I gripped the buggy with pure terror over what would happen if I fell and let go. Every walk resulted in me feeling sick and left me with hands that ached constantly from how tight I was gripping the handle. White-knuckle rollercoaster rides had nothing on me and my wintery buggy walks.

During these walks my little girl would be sleeping peacefully, blissfully unaware that her sleep-deprived mummy was fighting down the fear rising like bile in the back of her throat. I envisioned the buggy and my baby slipping from my vicelike grip and plummeting to her doom or a car losing its control and crashing into us on the pavement. So vivid and real a fear was this that I started to avoid walking along pavements on busy roads. Instead I chose the quieter roads that would take me safely down to the river running through our town. There, surrounded by silence, I would push myself and the buggy through the snow-laden paths: my tiny human was wrapped up warm and snuggly against the winter elements while I walked so hard I would finish drenched in sweat and fighting to catch my breath in the ice cold mountain air. Sweaty, but safe: mission accomplished. I'd managed yet another walk without causing the death of my baby. I could relax.

• Wanting to escape and outrun my mind

I now realise that walking through the snowy wilderness, my tiny human sleeping as I methodically trudged through or over snow drifts as fast as I could, was my form of escape. And when I say escape I actually mean it. It was my way of escaping from my mind – or at least was a determined attempt to outrun it. I felt tormented. I could never switch off. My mind was always racing. It was filled with random thoughts and fears, ranging from feeding schedules to sterilising bottles, from how best to rearrange the nursery drawers (for the tenth time that week) to how I was going to prevent the death of my baby. But whilst I was walking along the river, surrounded by nothing but white – snow-covered trees and glistening icicle-edged peace, – it was just me and my tiny human. I would get on that snowy path, my nose frozen, my heart starting to race, and I would push my legs and my body to move as fast as I could, as I tried to outrun the noise in my head – if only for a few moments. To run and get ahead of it, to set myself free, to escape and enjoy the silence.

I often wonder now what I must have looked like to passers-by (few and far between at that time of year; I was usually the only one literally crazy enough to be walking, let alone pushing a buggy). There we were, me with a grimaced look on my determined face, fully clad in winter gear, pushing the buggy like a demon, lost in my personal pursuit of silence as I manoeuvred us over whatever snowdrift was in our way. It must have been a strange sight!

I probably looked quite wild. To be honest, that is quite a good word to sum up my mental state at that time. I felt like a wild, untamed and unknown species. Something I didn't recognise but which I also understood completely.

During these early months of motherhood, my days were spent

trying to cage this wildness. Trying to tame it through the normal schedules and acts of everyday mum life. However, when no one was around, this wildness was left to run free and untamed, ruling my days with its unruliness whilst I watched on as a spectator of my own life.

• Unusual rituals

The days where I was alone and therefore able to indulge this wildness freely, saw me spending my days charged on empty adrenaline and feeling acute anxiety. As crazy as it sounds, it made me feel as if my senses were tuned into the universe and I was able to feel and hear everything around me as if we were one living organism. All my nerve endings were primed and on high alert and I would spend my days charging around the house, feeding, changing, cuddling and entertaining Éva.

I had the lounge set up in different sensory areas – reading, tummy time, soft play – and we would venture around each one. Then she would be fed and changed and placed down for her nap. Then I would begin the ritual of reorganising the lounge so all was ready for when she woke up. I would sterilise all the bottles, have two jugs filled with sterile water, as well as each bottle already filled with the correct amount of water and the formula measured out to precision in its container. I put the washing on, and dried and folded the clean laundry. Then I would clean everywhere and begin the daily stock take of the nappies, rearrange her clothes into size order, and place away any clothes she had outgrown. Once this part of my daily checklist had been completed I would try to have a quick shower, after which she would be waking from her morning nap and the whole play–feed–change ritual would start again. It exhausted and exhilarated me in equal measure. I was functioning on around one to two hours of sleep a night and spent my days veering from being supercharged and overefficient to depleted and desolate with no energy to smile, let alone get dressed and leave the house.

There was no middle ground for me, no mediocre, no calm and no let-up to this all consuming pattern. I was either the superefficient, super-sociable, supermum coping better than anyone else or so buried in the pits of despair and self-loathing that I stopped answering phone calls and texts and stopped leaving the house. My friends and family only ever got to see the supercharged me, the me who, despite being as tired as expected, was coping and had her mummy shit together.

• Loss of appetite

I'll always remember a good friend of mine asking me a few months after having Éva when I had lunch? Did I have it whilst Éva was awake or did I wait until I'd managed to get her down for a nap? I laughed at her, as I thought she was joking, and said, 'I don't have time to eat.' My friend was visibly shocked, realising that I was being serious and I wasn't actually eating. I asked her what now feels like a totally ludicrous question: 'Do *you* eat?'. At the time this was a serious question, no joke intended. I couldn't quite get my head around how she managed to eat, how she found the time to look after herself as well as her baby, and I wanted to learn how I could do this. It was then that it dawned on me that I couldn't remember the last time I felt hungry or the last meal I had prepared for myself whilst my husband wasn't there.

As I watched the concern sweep across my friend's face, a little voice inside me screamed: 'Stop talking! You're going to get into trouble.' I'd overshared. I'd revealed something that I obviously shouldn't have, so I quickly changed the direction of the conversation towards the more light-hearted, adding that I was 'too tired to remember my name let alone eat' and promising that I would start making more of an effort. I didn't. Things carried on right along as they were.

• The 'I'm coping' deception

One of the most destructive elements of a mental health illness is the secret nature of it. I quickly became an expert in 'I'm coping' deception. I would put on a show, a façade that I was coping. Yes, I was tired, but yes, I was most definitely coping and taking motherhood all in my stride. Tired but yes, most definitely happy. Naturally overwhelmed at times, but most definitely coping.

The outside world (and my husband to some extent in the early days) just saw me as Liv enjoying motherhood and doing a damn fine job of it. I said all the right things, thanks to all the candy-coated parenting magazines and blogs I'd read beforehand on how 'real mums' talk and act after having a baby. I did all the right activities, lived up to all the new mum clichés. I was in every sense and expectation of the outside world 'coping'.

Unfortunately, the only thing I was coping at was convincing everyone else (including myself at times) that I was OK.

I'll always remember a good friend being shocked to hear that I'd been diagnosed with PND. Out of all our friends with babies, she thought that I was the one 'coping best' at being a new mum.

I was not.

• Socialising

During the months following Éva's birth, I could still function in social situations. However, the energy it took for me to be able to build up my self-confidence and resolve to take part was monumental. From being a social butterfly who loved having friends round I came to dread the words, 'I've invited some mates over for dinner.' It zapped all my energy and sent my mind reeling and my anxiety levels soaring. Prior to any get-together I could always be found hiding out in our bathroom and psyching myself up to be able to face everyone, to get through the next few hours being the sociable and bubbly Liv that everyone expected.

The only person who got to see behind the veil and to be introduced to the two sides of my personality was my husband. It must have been so confusing to him at first, seeing me be the person he loved on one day and a total stranger the next. However, during the first several months, the erratic nature of my behaviour meant that it was easy to put the bad days down to one-offs; the next day I seemed OK again and back to myself. And so the vicious circle continued – me desperately ill and in need of help but also desperately convincing.

THE EFFECTS OF PND

I'd heard in the press about PND (linking the illness to mums being unable to feel maternal), but I didn't ever doubt my ability to take care of Éva. I never once doubted feeling maternal towards her. No matter how lost I felt and despite the darkest of days, I never once questioned if I was the best person to be looking after her. I was certain deep-down that I was the best person to look after her and that, no matter what happened to me or how desperate I felt, she would always be my top priority. She would always come first even at the sake of my own wellbeing. I loved her more than life itself.

By contrast, my relationship with my husband, Jamie, deteriorated.

• My relationship with my husband

I cannot describe how difficult it has been writing this next bit, but here goes . . .

It is one of the most difficult things to own up to, but at the time I resented my husband so deeply for not protecting me from what was happening. For carrying on as normal, inviting friends over, planning normal sociable things to do, whilst I was having the shit kicked out of me, mentally. For not realising how wrong things were, for not rescuing me from the terror that I was experiencing and enduring in silence. For not realising how much danger I was in. For not realising that I had given up everything to have his child.

We as a couple were being led down an incredibly dangerous and ugly path, and with each step my resentment for him grew stronger and the distance between us greater.

Just before I was diagnosed with PND, Jamie went away for a week cycling with one of his best friends. It had been a trip he'd had planned since before the birth. At the time of booking, it was a trip I was happy for him to take. I was going to use it as a good excuse to go home to the UK for a week with Éva, to see family and friends and then meet him at the finishing point in the UK.

If we had both known how ill I was, he would never have gone. However, he didn't, he just saw that his tired wife was being a bit of an arsehole at times, someone he no longer recognised, and he probably viewed the trip as a much-needed break. I, on the other hand, watched him leave and resented him for abandoning me and us at a time when I was at my most vulnerable and isolated. I remember Éva and I waving him off and feeling an incredible numbness take hold of my heart and a detachment from him. I thought: 'Well, there he goes, off for a week of freedom, doing something he loves most in the world whilst I am left here, on my own, holding the baby and trying to hold onto my grip on reality.'

I felt abandoned, uncared for and alone, and I hated him for it. As the week progressed, I flew us back to the UK (something I cannot even remember doing now) and visited family with Éva. The detachment I felt from him came with me. It was something I couldn't shake off; it had taken hold of me.

Unlike other times when we had been apart, I did not look forward to his phone calls. I did not try to keep in contact with him, and when he did call me with updates on his trip I was unenthusiastic to the point of not caring less. I was hurt, confused and resentful – and unfortunately he got it from both barrels.

This was the man I had once loved with every fibre of my person, but now I found myself looking at him like I had no clue who he even was. I wasn't a part of us anymore and felt immune to any feelings I'd had towards him previously.

Rather than being the welcoming wife, waving welcome home flags on his return, I missed him crossing the finishing line. I couldn't get my head around how little I cared about us and our relationship and, if I'm completely honest, how little I cared about anything at all – apart from Éva.

I can't begin to imagine what a total mind fuck it was for him. He was no longer living with his happy-go-lucky, enthusiastic wife who loved him to bits. Instead he was existing alongside an incredibly erratic and angry stranger who had cut herself off from him – and he had no idea why.

My lack of interest in us and my shutdown led him to ask the heartbreaking question: 'Liv, do you want a divorce?'.

He followed by asking if the reason I was so unhappy and so distant was because I no longer wanted to be with him. I told him that of course I didn't want a divorce and of course I still wanted to be with him. However, hand on heart, at that time, the illness had taken me over so completely and seeped its ugly waters into every part of my life that actually I felt no emotion at all when he asked what should have been a devastating question. If he'd walked out on me right there and then, I was so numb that I would have not felt anything at all.

These are pretty strong and ugly sentiments, particularly when it comes to talking about the love of my life – and the person who helped pull me through the darkness with his soul-strengthening promises that we were going to get through the hell we now found ourselves in.

A month later, I was diagnosed with PND. Without this diagnosis, our marriage would not have survived. I would have instead spiralled down further into the illness and my actions would have confirmed his greatest fear that I no longer wanted to be with him. It is a miracle any relationship survives through a battle with a mental illness, and after going through it ourselves as a couple we understand how relationships are destroyed because of it rather than made stronger. Sometimes love, family and a history together are not enough. Even the strongest and once happiest of relationships cannot survive the brutal and unforgiving damage it causes.

A mental illness rips out the very heart and soul of a partnership. It knocks down the little kingdom and safe haven you have created together, leaving a path of mangled and charred remains in its wake. Once you have endured this destruction, it is time to try and rebuild a new city of hope together, one that can house you and your family safely. Unfortunately, for some this is impossible. They do not make it through to the other side. The damage done is irreversible; there is nothing left to rebuild, no desire left to try again. There is no going back, there is no going forward, no happy ending.

Like all love stories, ours has had its share of happiness, challenges, heartbreak and darkness to overcome. Stuff like this, we thought, wasn't supposed to happen to a couple like us. We were supposed to be strong enough, positive enough, happy enough for our lives not to be blighted by an illness that took us over the cliff of our relationship and into the mouth of hell.

However, it did happen to us, we were not immune to it. And why should we have been? Because you know what I've learned? No one is immune. I am proud and at times in awe at the things we have overcome, the depths we have sometimes managed to drag ourselves up from – and I look back in disbelief at the unapologetic grit and blind determination it took to stay together through it all.

But together we still are. In some ways, a little weaker and unhealed in places, the precipice too wide still to cross. We live with the hard but honest truth that we as a couple are not (as we once thought when standing in a beautiful château grounds in front of all our family and friends) unbreakable. But we are in many ways stronger than we ever thought possible.

We have not quite found our happy ever after. There are still wounds trying to heal and memories that need to be more distant than they are currently. But somehow we are back on our path. We know, without speaking of them, the things that have cemented us together. The dark corners to which we have journeyed. The demons we have faced and overthrown. And we know that when the going got tougher than we ever dreamed possible, we have been there for each other – for better and for worse.

That to me makes ours a love story and a half. That is where the true, honest and challenging romance lies. That is what I find more romantic than candlelit dinners; the strength, pure grit and determination it took to survive, to keep surviving and to forge the next part of our journey battle wounded, but together.

THE TIPPING POINT – GETTING DIAGNOSED

Being ill with PND strips you of any sense of control – over your life, your mind and your emotions. It's this lack of control that can send you spiralling deeper into the illness without knowing if there is any way back. For me, this lack of control destroyed the very core of who I was. I, therefore, clung onto the one and only bit of control I felt I had left: the control over the daily *Mummy's Got Her Shit Together Show*. Oh yes, as long as I was in control of how others perceived me as a new mum and as long as I could control the 'together and coping' impression of me the outside world was seeing, then it didn't matter that I was losing my mind behind closed doors.

I came to discover the truth – which is as unavoidable as it is inevitable – that this 'control' cannot and does not last forever. Like a bad TV show, the *Mummy's Got Her Shit Together Show* was decommissioned; no follow-up series was wanted. You see, this form of control is short-lived – and, as I found out, it finally screws you over royally! After several months of trying to keep my show together and trying to carry on as normal, my control up and left and I had a complete breakdown.

What was my tipping point I hear you ask? What was the big

moment that sent this control packing? Nappies. Yes, nappies, and the fact that we were a pack of Size 4 nappies down.

Let me explain Nappygate to you.

I had drawers and cupboards filled to the brim with nappies, all organised in order of size and calculated down to the last change and the time when she would need the next size. (Hello OCD, so glad you could join the party!) I had the wardrobe drawers packed with the 'soon to be needed nappies', all in size order, and then her 'wearing now' drawers packed with nappies the right size for her at the time. (I had the same rota with her clothes and toys too; I would have made a fantastic librarian!)

I would visit the drawers daily and run my hand over the neatly packed and organised array of nappies, packs of wipes, muslins, multiple jars of Vix and bottles of 'just in case' Calpol, neatly folded and organised vests, Baby-gros, outfits and matching socks – and I would feel a sense of fulfilment and achievement. A feeling that despite the negative sentiments of my mind, I was in fact a good mum. These drawers and their ridiculous level of organisation were the proof. If I was having a really bad day, I just had to look into these drawers to prove I was a good mum, I'd done my little girl proud. I deserved her.

However, on the day of Nappygate, I opened the drawers of the wardrobe to find that it wasn't brimming with nappies like it should have been. There was a whole row missing of Size 4 nappies. (I should probably add that she was only in size 2s at the time and was tiny for her age, so she was probably not going to be in this size for a good few months to come.)

I quickly and desperately checked inside the main wardrobe for the back up 'future packs' – and there were none. Panic gripped me like nothing I have ever known, my final strand of logic and common sense left the building and I was tipped over the edge and into the ravine of the illness; no control, no holds barred, no coming back. I instead found myself fully immersed in the murky depths. I could take no more.

My hubby came into the nursery to find me holding our tiny human and hysterical. My 'I'm coping' mask had not just slipped off; it was lying in tatters on the nursery floor and there was no longer any more disguising the wreck that, until this moment, had been hiding beneath it.

Everything came rushing to the surface and I told him:

'I can't do this.'

'I think I'm going crazy.'

'I can't handle this anymore.'

'I'm having a breakdown.'

'I need help.'

'Please help me.'

With the release of these words and my fears, I felt as though I had been set free. Finally I was allowing myself to give in to what was happening to me in all its ugly glory. It was terrifying and at the same time an incredible relief to finally own the fact that I was ill. That I was in trouble. That I was so desperate for help.

I look back now and think of this as my first step, my first moment of taking charge amidst the chaos. Breaking down and admitting my illness to my husband gave me a small but real bit of control over this freewheeling juggernaut that was taking me off road, to places I didn't want to know about, let alone visit.

With my husband's support, I made an appointment to see the doctor the next day. It was probably one of the hardest steps I had to take to get well again. Thanks to my lack of knowledge about the illness and what was happening to me, I was consumed with the fear that admitting I was unwell to a professional would mean I would be labelled as an unfit mother and have my baby taken from me. In reality, the conversation with my doctor was straightforward and undramatic. I told him what I was going through and cried; he confirmed that he thought I had Postnatal Depression, prescribed me with a course of anti-depressants and advised me on the types of counselling available. He wanted to monitor my progress, so we booked a follow-up appointment in two weeks' time – and I was sent on my way, very relieved. Relieved that I was fighting an illness that now had a name, relieved that there hadn't been any mention or hint of my being an unfit mum or any chance of my baby being taken away from me.

That said, with the beauty of hindsight after going through something so ugly, I can now see that my recovery would have been quicker if the approach to its treatment had been more rounded and substantial. If I had been handed a leaflet detailing what the illness was, the warning signs, the treatment options, where to get help locally, where to get support for my husband who was now my carer – just one leaflet, and we would have been set up as a much stronger unit, more able for the battle that now lay ahead of us.

However, I had taken the first vital step. I had admitted I was unwell. And by doing so, I was owning my illness rather than it owning me. I now just had to start taking the pills and start kicking its ass.

CHAPTER 6

THE EVERY MUM GUIDE TO POSTNATAL DEPRESSION

So let's get straight down to business, shall we?

PND is a TOTAL MOTHERFUCKER.

Let's just sit and let these words sink in for a moment . . .

PND is a TOTAL MOTHERFUCKER.

It enters our world unannounced and uninvited during the most inconvenient time of our lives (aka the moment after a tiny human has exited our body). It doesn't care less how exhausted we are, the type of birth we've had, the fact that we are trying to look after our new tiny human as best we can, or what a lovely, fun and optimistic person we normally happen to be. Oh no, the only thing this illness cares about is finding a way in, taking hold of us and doing all it can to well and truly mess up any previous plans and thoughts we had on what motherhood was going to be like.

The not so funny part in this not so funny tale is that the lack of awareness of the illness and its symptoms – and the stigma surrounding maternal mental health illnesses – means that we (ourselves and our partners) are quite simply not prepared to deal with such a cruel, vicious visitor bursting the bubble of what should be – and what we have been sold as being – one of the best and most precious times of our lives.

Yes, we have heard about feeding options, birth plans and sleep schedules until we have them coming out of our ears. We are 100 per cent clued up on the latest buggies, car seats and cot beds. Hell, we even now know about how to tone and strengthen our pelvic floor. However, postnatal depression – or even the fact that we should be paying attention to our maternal mental health, both pre- and post-baby – doesn't even get a place at the pregnancy party.

I am here to call time on this nonsense and the downright damaging silence that surrounds this illness. And instead to speak openly about the key things I wish I had known when facing motherhood for the first time as a mum with a maternal mental health illness. The things that I wish I could have read somewhere during my lowest and darkest of days, to help me address my fears and reassure me that I was not alone in what I was going through.

• It's not your fault

I know everything feels like your fault at the moment. I know you feel as though you have done something to cause the illness or have done something to deserve it. You feel useless. You feel inconsequential. You feel you are not enough. But if you take only one thing from reading this book, please take this: You haven't done anything to deserve this. You have done nothing to cause it. It is not your fault.

• You are NOT a bad mum

Yes, I know you have an overwhelming belief that you are. I know you are questioning every thought, every feeling, look and decision you are making. I know you feel as if your tiny human deserves better. That they deserve someone who can love them and look after them properly. Someone who knows better, who is better qualified, who is just – more. Listen to me and *listen good!*

YOU ARE NOT A BAD MUM!

You have been dealt a really shitty card. Alongside bringing a tiny human into this world and dealing with everything this gargantuan task has thrown at you, you have also been landed with a cruel and thought-less illness. An illness that no one can see but which is tearing you apart inside and leaving you feeling lost, isolated, vulnerable and petrified. It is taking hold, whispering untruths into your heart, filling you with dread and giving weight to the lie that you are an 'unfit mother'.

I've been there. I know the struggle and the battle you are facing. What I didn't know at the time of my darkest of days was that it was the illness telling me these things. It was the illness lying to me with such force and perseverance that before long I took on these poisonous thoughts and devastating beliefs as my own.

I am here to remind you that your illness is lying to you. Your illness is deceiving you. I know it's damn near impossible to ignore the persistent voice of your illness. However, when that voice gets too loud, too intrusive, too easy to believe, when you start to believe the voice is your own, come back here and read these words and listen to my voice instead telling you:

YOU ARE A GOOD MUM!

• *Your tiny human does not think you're a fake or a phoney*

One of my biggest beliefs and fears after having my eldest daughter was that despite her being just weeks old; despite her not being able to speak yet; despite her newness and limited knowledge of this new world she now found herself in − the one thing she did know was that I was a phoney. A fake mum. It was only a matter of time before everyone else found out and rescued her from me and placed her into the arms of the real mum that she deserved.

I watched my daughter watching me, following my every move and sound. She looked at me with her beautiful big blue eyes and it was as though she was looking beyond the fake exterior of a mum who was coping, the hollow new mum smiles which the rest of the world (including her daddy) had fallen for, and was giving me a look that meant 'I'm not buying it. You are not fooling me! Where is my real mum? How did I end up with this dud instead?'.

I believed that my tiny human knew I was a fake, a phoney, a crap mum. I wanted to scream, 'Why can't anyone else see the truth? Someone needs to save her from me and give her to a mum she deserves.'

The level of insecurity, anxiety and self-loathing this illness can instil in us is as terrifying as it is debilitating. We are left believing that the one person we love most and wanted most in the world, the one tiny person we have been dreaming of meeting for what feels like forever, the one person we want to hold, to love, to nurture is the one person who does not want us, the one person who deserves better than what we have to offer.

It is only now in hindsight that I realise I got it wrong. It is only now that I realise, without the dark veil of PND blurring my vision, that what she was really trying to tell me was something quite different.

Remembering how she looked at me, I now realise that rather than questioning me she was actually trying to reassure me, and was saying:

'I see your hurt. I understand. Don't worry, it's all going to be OK as long as we have each other. I love you mummy. You are my world.'

I know this now because I am well once more. I know this now because I no longer have a dark passenger barraging me with evil and spiteful untruths, trying to turn me against myself. God, it is a bloody ferocious battle to make yourself believe that your tiny human does love you, that they DO want you as their mummy. That they don't think you're a phoney. That they don't want anybody else apart from you. That all they want is you their amazing mummy. End of. But this is the truth.

So next time you find your tiny human looking into your eyes and you start to hear the familiar sound of insecurities and doubts seeping in, just remember that what they are really trying to say to you is;

'I love you mummy. You are my world.'

• Find your fight

When we are suffering from a maternal mental health illness that controls us and has such a strong hold over us, one of the worst fears and beliefs is that it now owns us. We are no longer in charge and we no longer have the ability to determine where our life and our minds are heading.

I felt at a total loss throughout the early parts of my illness, not knowing why I felt the way I did, feeling as though I had no control over what it was doing to my life or any strength to tackle it. However, this is when something clicked in me. I started to view my illness as something I had to fight. This gave a physicality to the illness, and made me able to visualise the illness as a person. A person who had invaded my life and whom I now had to fight to reclaim my life and my mind. I found my fight, which enabled me to find the strength for the battle I had every day. Now I had the fire in my belly to face up to my illness and to do all I could to overcome it.

• Anti-depressants are NOTHING to be ashamed of!

'It's just a pill. If you had a headache, you would take a tablet to make it better. This is just the same as that!'

'No, it bloody isn't,' I screamed back at my husband, who was trying to convince me not to feel ashamed about having to take anti-depressants. 'Give me a headache any day over my mind being fucked up.'

God, I hated the fact and despised myself that things had got so bad that I was now a new mum having to pop pills to get through the day. How the eff did this happen to me? I was so angry! I was supposed to be happy. I was supposed to be well. I was supposed to be loving my life, and here I was instead about to place the responsibility for all these things onto a tiny pill sitting on my tongue and waiting to be swallowed.

Was this going to take me on a slippery slope to all things mental? Was I going to become addicted to them and, before you know it, be sectioned and strapped down in a padded room with electrodes on my head and no idea where my baby or new family were?

It was scary trying to reason with my unreasonable mind that my hubby was right, that it was just a pill and I needed it to make me feel better.

I ended up screaming to myself repeatedly: 'Just take the fucking pill! Just take the fucking pill! JUST TAKE THE F'ING PILL! *TAKE IT!*'.

So I did.

I took the fucking pill and kept taking them until they started to make me feel better. They gave me the first chance of seeing a way out. They helped to clear a corner amongst all the evil crap in my mind, a place where I could sit, take stock and make a plan as to how I was going to start to clear the rest of the crap out. They gave me a respite from the illness, where I could gather my thoughts, my energy reserves, my troops, to come back fighting and to kick the illness into touch. They gave me my first glimmer of hope that I could feel well again.

So, if you are finding yourself in the same shame-filled predicament I did, just you remember this:
Screw the shame. Screw feeling you've failed. Screw being ill. Take the fucking pill!

• You need to get help

This illness is not going to go away without any help or support. The level of help and support you will need to get through PND will depend on just how ill it is making you feel. But regardless of whether you have mild or severe symptoms, you do need a helping hand in your personal battle.

I have spoken a lot to women about my own experiences of PND and postnatal psychosis. In fact, it's got to the point now where I am comfortable enough to drop the fact that I suffered into conversations with mums at the park or on playdates – and I have been overwhelmed by the number of mums who have then opened up to me about their own experiences. A number of women have said: 'I'm sure I had something like that after having my children, but I never went for help, so I'm not sure if it was PND or not. Something was definitely wrong and, to be honest, I still suffer with things today.' It is heartbreaking to hear of other mums suffering – even more so to hear of a mum who has suffered without help.

Addressing this illness, no matter what form it takes, is vital. If the issues are not addressed and dealt with properly, they can have lasting negative effects, which we can carry around long after we have given birth and our tiny humans have grown. And who wants that? I know I don't want to be carrying around the burden of depression for the rest of my life. I don't want its evil creeping into even more areas of my life.

Back then I wanted control back. I wanted a chance to be completely well again and to be allowed to enjoy motherhood. Getting help was my first step towards this.

• Find the right route for you

Help for me took a variety of forms. My winning combination was the rock solid and constant support from my husband, a course of anti-depressants, counselling and letting my friends and family know that I was suffering. I also started to share my experiences by writing articles about my illness, and publishing them on my Facebook page, blog and other online sites. My writing became a form of therapy for me; it allowed me to give a voice to my illness and to share my personal insight into living with a maternal mental health illness.

After I published my early articles, I received messages from other mums going through the same thing, and I am still in touch with some of these mums today. Being able to write about my experiences, and then to receive messages from other mums who had been or were going through the same thing, made me realise I was not alone and that it was something that needed to be spoken about more. The route out of the illness is different for everyone – but once you find your first step on that path, you can start to look ahead and realise there is a way out.

In some of my most darkest of times, it took a hell of a lot of perseverance to stay on that path. However, slowly but surely, it led me to where I am today – well and reclaiming my right to enjoy motherhood.

CHAPTER 7

POPPING YOUR MOTHERHOOD CHERRY

As well as battling a number of 'firsts' that came from being a mum whose mental health was suffering, I was also popping my motherhood cherry, and going through all the 'normal' firsts – those crazy, hilarious and exhausting experiences that every new mum goes through.

When we become a mum, we find ourselves in a hazy world of firsts that can make us feel empowered and in control on the good days – and slightly off kilter and unhinged on the not so good days, when minimal sleep and never having done this before makes everything seems like an uphill struggle, and you have no clue even about where you are struggling to go.

So, my lovely friend, I am here to talk motherhood firsts. And to share a few little gems I wish someone had given me when I was popping my motherhood cherry.

FIRST POST-BABY POO – 'I'M SHIT SCARED TO TAKE A SHIT'

Just when you thought you had fulfilled your quota of terrifying acts by bringing a tiny human into this world kicking and screaming, you are then faced with a task so horrific that you would prefer to be back in the labour room. It was scary enough having to push out a baby. Now the ante has been upped by the request that you push out your first post–baby poo.

Terrified does not even come close to the feelings of dread that overwhelm your exhausted and pain-riddled body at the request from your midwife (who at this point resembles a pointy eye browed, turd demanding heathen): 'Have you had a poo yet?'.

Holy Mother of God, is she for real?

You have been ripped to shreds and sewn back up and now you have to try and squeeze out a poo? How about it feels like they have mistakenly sewn up all exits down there? How about the pressure will split me front to back and I'll have to live the rest of my days going to the toilet in a plastic bag attached to my stomach? Not a chance in hell am I putting myself through that, no matter how desperate I get for a poo. Unlike my baby, it is going to have to stay put. I am taking back control.

This longed-for control lasts a whole ten minutes before Sod's Law kicks in: which means that the moment you start thinking about not having something, then along that something comes and any control you had is out the window and down the toilet. Accompanied by your sobbing tears of terror as you inform your partner: 'I just can't do this, I'm too scared, it's going to hurt so much.'

Oh yes, ladies, the run-up to labour has nothing on this!

Why do we not warn unsuspecting mums to be that we go from worrying about pooing ourselves during birth to eventually wishing we had in order to prolong the interval before we need to go afterwards? When thinking about the pain and fear of having a tiny human, our brains stop in the labour room and do not think past the moment of said tiny human's arrival. So when these post-baby moments happen to you, you feel completely cheated and totally unprepared.

I am not too scared to talk about poo. It is now commonplace in my everyday life and on some days (the really bad ones) it has become part of my everyday wardrobe – the random smudge on the cuff of my sleeve, the odd streak on the side of my jeans, and most disgustingly a smear across my top lip. So my friend, the truth of the matter is, poo – and its bezzies, puke and snot – are going to be a big part of your life, the mother of all introductions being the first poo you have after giving birth.

Fear not, unlike most experiences of childbirth, the actual reality of having a post-baby poo is nowhere near as bad as the thought of it. Despite thinking the midwife needs either a punch in the face or muzzling when she encourages you to push as hard as you can, the truth is, the woman is right. You can, and it is not as painful as you fear. The only thing you may feel is a twinge of embarrassment when you remember that you cried about taking a dump!

Any chance of a silver lining? I hear you ask. Just remind yourself that you will at least be able to sympathise with your distraught child when they have to do the same during potty training. However (unfortunately, for them) they will be being filmed in front of an encouraging audience and sat on a piece of brightly coloured plastic. Somehow, your predicament now seems a lot less barbaric.

LEAVING HOSPITAL FOR THE FIRST TIME

Run for your lives, before 'they' change their minds.

You've actually gone and done it. You've fooled, I mean convinced them into allowing you to leave the hospital, the safe and cosy domain where you are cocooned away from the big bad world of parenthood. They actually think you are grown-up enough to look after a baby.

'It worked! They think we are responsible enough to take her home!'

The first incredulous words I said to my husband after being told we could leave the hospital with our tiny human.

'They believed us, they think we are grown up enough to take care of her.'

We could take her home. They were letting us take her home. Had these fools gone mad?!?

Leaving the bubble of the hospital, no matter how long or short your stay, feels a bit like breaking the law. You are leaving the building with a precious item in tow, hoping to God you don't drop them in front of the gathering onlookers and feeling that at any minute an alarm is going to get triggered as the hospital staff realise you're leaving with the baby and that they've made a terrible mistake.

Despite the baby being yours and despite loving this new little being with all your heart, you still can't grasp the fact they have been crazy enough to let you home without a chaperone. Don't they need to call our parents or bosses for references?

No alarm is triggered and no strong arm of the hospital security stands in your way. Instead you find yourselves stepping out of those revolving doors, with your precious little one bundled up in way too many clothes, three hats, oversized mittens and under a dozen blankets (despite it being mid-June and 25°C), and you grinning like Cheshire cats on speed. A grin that slowly dissipates into a hysterical grimace with each step away from the bosom of the professionals as you realise that, holy hell, the rest is now over to you. Every decision. Every moment. Every day. Forever.

Are you freaking out yet? I know I was!

As the road of their tiny lives flashes before your eyes, so does the panic and you find your feet heading back to the hospital doors.

Don't worry . . . Seriously! You have got this!

Take a deep breath, keep putting one foot in front of the other, and be sure to capture the moment so you can look back proudly in several months' time at the new parents, with their terrified grins, looking more like Bambi on ice rather than the veteran and awesome parents you have now become.

'WHAT DO WE DO WITH IT WHEN WE GET IT HOME?'

Home safely? Check! Still breathing? Check! Nappy changed? Check! Still breathing? Check! Fed? Check! Still breathing? Check!

OK, so, what the hell do we do next?

Something happens as you take that drive home from the hospital with your new tiny human on board. As the hospital slowly disappears into the distance, so does any information you have learnt about how to keep this new tiny human alive and happy. You may have listened intently, feeling you are leaving as a fount of new baby knowledge, but the moment you hear the clunk of the car seat, a secondary clunk follows. That secondary clunk is the sound of your brain tipping over and dispelling any baby info you've learnt out of your ear and onto the pavement. Unfortunately, you and your partner are too busy debating over whether or not the straps of the car seat are pulled tightly enough to realise. Instead, you take your virgin voyage home under a sunny cloud of optimism, whilst your brain is sat curb side screaming;

'Wait, you fools! You're gonna need me!!!'.

Please try not to panic. This is all part of the new parent winging it, and soon enough you will come to realise that winging it is one of the key prerequisites to becoming a parent. Hell, you can even now buy cool sweatshirts that proudly proclaim just this. (BIG shout out to the awesome Selfish Mother Sweatshirts.)

When you finally make it home (at a speed of 10 mph), you soon realise this: that even though you have lived in your house for a million years and made a trillion happy memories within its walls, when you enter your home with your new tiny human you are seeing it for the first time. The beautiful, must-have home accessories are now baby deathtraps, and the luxury cream Mongolian rug, which no one dare set foot on pre-baby, is now looking like the perfect play mat.

I remember arriving home for the first time with our eldest tiny human and placing her on the kitchen island in her car seat. She was sleeping soundly, without a care in the world, whilst me and the hubby ran around like deranged nutbags trying to figure out where we should put the Moses basket, the change mat and whether or not we should wake her up to 'show her around her new home'.

Should we wake up our soundly sleeping newborn? What the hell were we thinking? And so the games began . . . We woke up our soundly sleeping newborn and then had to call it quits on the grand tour because she was now screaming for her milk and wondering why the hell she was not still soundly asleep. Those first days back at home with our new tiny human, everything felt so brand new. I would find myself wandering around her nursery, looking at all the clothes I had packed away in the drawers and all the baby gadgets we had spent months collecting and thinking, 'Wow, they are no longer just things. They actually have a purpose and are going to be used by our daughter'. Such a crazy, surreal and lovely realisation that all the things that, pre-baby, were exciting things to tick off the list were now things that were going to be a part of our new normal life.

I promise you, give it a week and everything will feel normal. You will be changing your tiny human's pooey bum on the sofa, the Moses basket will be a permanent fixture in whatever room you are in at the time and you will never, ever think it's a good idea to wake a sleeping baby. Ever!

THE FIRST TIME A STRANGER ASKS AFTER THE WELFARE OF YOUR FANNY

When you imagined the moment you announced the birth of your child, did you ever imagine that after the standard query of name and weight, the burning question on people's lips, would be asking about your fanny and how many stitches you had to endure? No? Funny, that — me neither.

Two tiny humans in and I'm still baffled as to (a) why anyone would want to know this about their own fanny, let alone anyone else's; and (b) how anyone is brave enough to ask about the state of someone else's fanny in the first place?

I'm curious about what people do with the information when they have managed to glean it from an unprepared and *shocked to be talking about her fanny with a work colleague* mum. Is there a new stitch and bitch trend going around on social media I don't know about? Or are we all being entered into a who's who of vaginas that are more patchwork quilt than fanny?

I remember the first time my post-baby vagina was a topic of conversation. It was after the birth of my first tiny human and I was trying to get her to feed. A friend of a friend twice removed asked, 'Soooooo, how is she feeding? Oh and more importantly how many stitches did you have?'.

Bang! No messing. No skirting around the proverbial bush. Straight for the vagina jugular.

My poor vagina winced at the memory of the whole thing as I answered, 'Urgggh I'm not sure, I don't really know'. To this day I still don't know. In fact, I'm quite happy I don't. Following the birth of my eldest, I was so out of it that they could have been sewing on an elephant's trunk down here and I wouldn't have cared less.

That may have been the first time I got asked about the welfare of my nether regions, but it most certainly wasn't the last. And it didn't matter where I was or who was asking – apparently me and the state of my vagina was fair game and up for debate with a whole host of people, ranging from over-friendly acquaintances to people I'd never met before, all discussing my nether regions and how they were recovering like they were chatting about the weather. 'Ooh, lovely day today, so pleased the sun is out, how's your fanny?'

I would just like to say: Forgive me, but just because I've pushed a tiny human out of it, does not mean I now want to discuss how my vagina looks or feels with anyone, let alone the daughter of my

Aunty Mary's neighbour, whom I haven't seen since I was four and sitting in a bucket of water in the garden during a balmy British heatwave. I don't want to be part of *The Fanny Files*. As far as I'm concerned, we have to lose all sense of inhibitions and privacy when giving birth and I am OK with this. However, I'm afraid I'm not OK with it when fully dressed and in the local shop getting a pint of milk. (Obviously, writing about it here doesn't count. You aren't going to tell anyone, right?)

THE FIRST TIME YOU LEAVE YOUR TINY HUMAN

Like ripping off a Band-Aid that has been plastered onto your skin for a day too long, leaving your baby with someone else for the first time is scary and cold sweat inducing as you wonder if you can actually go through with it. Then you feel ridiculous because of course you should be feeling grateful for a break and then you feel racked with guilt for being grateful for being away from your tiny human. And so the guilt merry-go-round commences. Roll up, roll up! Tickets please, all aboard!

Whether you are leaving them for ten minutes or ten hours, whether they are aged ten days, ten months or ten years, the feelings of guilt and anxiety are palpable as you battle with your rational mind on one hand and your steroid-enhanced emotions on the other. One tells you nothing bad will happen and that a break will do you good, the other accuses you of abandoning your defenseless tiny human and being totally selfish. Even, if you do happen to be abandoning them with their adoring grandparents and not in a shopping basket on the side of the road, the result is the same.

I remember the first time my husband and I left our eldest to go for a meal out together. She was a few months old. My parents were visiting us and I had psyched myself up that I was going to be OK leaving her and that I wasn't a bad mum for doing so. We had booked into a lovely restaurant just a short walk away from home and I had got myself showered and dressed in something other than the maternity leggings and jumper that had become my staple outfit. I felt good. I was going to enjoy my night with my husband. However, every step I took away from the house I felt a knot tighten in my stomach. I started to feel anxious and couldn't get over the physical effect that leaving her had on me. However, I also knew that having some time for just Jamie and myself was also important, and that since we were living in France these moments of child care were going to be few and far between, so we needed to take them whilst we could.

I managed to get through the meal with only a few phone calls and texts back home – to be told that she was sleeping and everything was fine (obviously) – and when we got home a couple of hours later, she was still sleeping and everything was still fine (obviously). However, throughout the whole meal I couldn't shake the feeling that I should be home looking after her rather than out enjoying a meal (which I had been looking forward to) and I started to feel guilty.

It's crazy, isn't it, that as much as you are longing for a bit of 'me-time', the moment you actually get it you then beat yourself up for having it and long to be back with your tiny human. So go easy on yourself. Whether you are feeling confident about leaving them or not, it's important to remember that you are also important. That there was a you before there was a them and that sometimes amongst the magic and mayhem of being a mum you need to feel like 'you' again. A bit of time to yourself can help you remember this.

SLEEP DEPRIVATION – OH SLEEP, WHEN WILL YOU BE MINE ONCE MORE?

Two additional and equally delightful elements of new motherhood I experienced were the ever so distressing facts that:

1. I was never going to sleep again. Ever;

and, when I finally did sleep,

2. Mummy guilt would ensure that my shuteye was more panicked
   than peaceful.

Let's start with the whole sleep thing, shall we?

I love my sleep. I love my bed. Pre-motherhood, 10 a.m. (on a
weekend) was getting up early. I have even been known (mainly
in my student days) to conduct whole days, including meals, from
the comfort of my own glorious, sleep-inducing, comfy as hell,
bed. Therefore, the whole not sleeping thing, which we all have to
endure after becoming a mum, didn't go down that well. In fact, it
turned me into a sleep obsessive demon, lusting after anything that
resembled a bit of shuteye. (I was not a pretty sight – ask my hubby.)
Our first tiny human was quite good at the whole sleeping thing: she
would go down for her naps easily and when we first brought her
home she was waking up every four hours for a feed. However, my
second tiny human was not so much of a fan of the whole napping,
resting or sleeping thing in general – and that drove me to the edge
of delirium. One week straight of her waking every hour, night and
day, for a feed, not wanting to sleep anywhere but on me (for which
my eighteen-month-old toddler then spent the majority of the day
screaming at me) and let's just say I was on the edge . . . the edge
of wanting to sleep anywhere even if it meant crawling up my own
areshole to grab forty winks. So on edge that I just had to write about
it and share my hell with every other mum going through the same.

What I wrote went something like this;

I'm *SO* Tired I Want to Crawl Up My Own Arse for a Nap

*I am so tired I want to crawl up my own arse and have a nap. Yes, not the
first place that springs to everyone's mind as a retreat of choice. However, I*

need somewhere, dark and uncrowded and, most importantly, somewhere no one (namely my tiny humans) would ever think I would be.

Ladies, I give you my arsehole. The one place I will surely be safe from the screams and demands of a tiny toddler, the wails of a hungry newborn (who surely cannot STILL be hungry after being attached to my boob 24/7) and the forever growing washing pile and sticky-fingered windows I can no longer see out of, let alone summon up the energy to be arsed to wipe clean.

Please someone, anyone, tell me when will this rational thought destroying and soul-sucking fatigue end?! When will there be a difference between night and day? When will I stop telling the time by how much my boobs resemble small heads wearing tiny brown hats? And when, oh when, will my bottom stop looking like a good place to stick my head up?!

I want (no, screw that), I NEED to know that there is an end to this torture. That my life, currently made up of never-ending nights and fuzzy days, will at some point start to resemble something of my previous one. A life where 4 a.m. is not a lie-in. In fact, a life where 4 a.m. can go fuck itself completely unless it involves me dancing my arse off under neon lights after enjoying copious amounts of overpriced yet deliciously potent cocktails. That is the only way 4 a.m. should EVER exist in my consciousness.

Please tell me this. How the hell am I supposed to be able to keep myself, let alone a tiny human alive and safe, if I don't even have the energy to remember my own name, let alone the time of the last feed or where the hell I put the 2 a.m. nappy? I am sure the late night poo parcel will turn up eventually . . . no doubt signalled by an overwhelming urge to retch as I catch an unexpected nose full of the eau de turd my little one has perfected.

The life of a mum of a newborn and, let's face it, of any sleep-depriving demon commonly known as our offspring, is one that stretches out before us in one continuous fug (aka fuzzy fog) of feeds, dirty nappies, swollen boobs, sterilising and pacing the hallway all whilst *fighting murderous urges towards your snoring partner. Oh, if you just had the energy to weight down that pillow over his smugly sleeping face. (Oh yes, nothing quite like the 2 a.m., sleep-deprived rage of a new mum.)*

Lack of sleep, and lusting after a full unbroken four hours of it, consumes our every waking thought, which due to the nature of the bitch that is sleepless nights means we are consumed by it 24/7. We post about it on Facebook, discuss it on forums, resent those getting it and plead to anyone who will listen to share any pearls of wisdom on how to get our little ones to sleep for longer than two lousy hours at a time.

Oh, the golden chalice of a four-hourly schedule. The joy of a 6.30 a.m. lie-in. The dare I say it (for fear it won't ever happen) unadulterated pleasure of being able to get into bed knowing you will not have to be out of it for a blissful seven hours. When, oh when, will you be mine?

I tell you when. 'Who the fuck knows o'clock' is when.

In the meantime, peeps, you know where to find me . . .

THE EVERY MUM GUIDE TO MUMMY GUILT

(TO BE READ WHEN YOU NEED TO GIVE MUMMY GUILT A BIG KICK IN THE ARSE)

We spend nine months trying to live like organic angels verging on born-again virgins, doing everything we can to grow a healthy tiny human. Buying into every miracle cream, vitamin and birthing class and book going. What keeps us committed through all the dry parties, the charcoaled steaks and inedible, non-runny eggs?

The thought that we are doing all we can to give our little ones the best start in life and that once we have completed our mission of growing and bringing a healthy tiny human into this world we can then ease off the pressure, give ourselves a huge pat on the back and enjoy our baby and all the things that make us feel normal and part of society at large.

Pah! Who were we kidding?!

Why does no one warn us that pregnancy is just the tip of the mummy guilt-laden iceberg and that once you actually reach motherhood status you will be living as a nervous wreck, feeling guilty about everything you think, feel, say, do, don't do, think about doing, never get round to doing, wish you could be doing, what you feel you should be thinking, feeling, saying, doing . . . ? It is bloody exhausting.

Ladies, I give you motherhood. The one thing capable of sending you from feeling like a million dollars to a piece of dog turd in one fatal swipe of a muslin cloth. It is a constant battle between our pre-baby self and our new mum self, a woman we don't quite recognise and with whom we are not familiar. However, here she is, as bold as brass, shoehorning herself into our consciousness and leaving us feeling guilty and anxious over the most ridiculous of things that would never even have registered with our former selves.

We've all been there, and most of us are there daily.

Let's say you are having one of the best days since labour day. You wake up after three hours of unbroken sleep (which now constitutes a full night's sleep), your little one is actually feeding to schedule and you've managed to have a shower – yes, an actual shower – and all before midday. You are feeling bloody amazing. You have this motherhood game down. Then wham bam! The arse that is mummy guilt comes sweeping in and slaps you round the face, throwing you off kilter and making you feel like a terrible mum.

Let the battle commence.

In one corner is your pre-mum self, telling you to get a grip, it's only a dummy/bottle/dirty nappy/glass of wine/night out/formula (the list goes on). You have nothing to feel guilty about. You are doing a great job. In the other corner sits the gut-twisting mum guilt, screaming at you that you can do better, undoing all your previous good work and leaving you a guilt-ridden, crumpled mess as you try to soothe a screaming baby whilst feeling like the worst mum in the world and questioning why the hell you thought you could pull it off in the first place?

And all this before you even dare contemplate your other worries of not spending enough time with any other children you may have. Of not having had sex or even a non-baby related conversation with your partner for what seems like a lifetime. Of knowing that all body parts north of your navel are more *Planet of the Apes* than yummy mummy.

We all stand guilty as charged.

On a daily basis us mums have two battles on our hands. One battle to get to bedtime all alive and in one piece and the other, never-ending battle with ourselves and the guilt that at times can be so debilitating we just want to throw in the towel and say to hell with it. Guilt trip, you win. I will now berate myself. I will now be a slave to the master that is mummy guilt. I surrender.

Ladies, do not be beaten; you do have this motherhood thing sorted. How do I know this? I am there with you. I, like the rest of you am juggling babies, my sanity and incessant guilt trips daily. And you know what made me take a step back and give myself a break? My tiny humans. Following the birth of our second daughter, I found myself mid-meltdown to my husband about not feeling like a good enough mum, when something caught my eye that stopped me and my guilt-laden tears in their tracks. Something so powerful that any guilt I felt was replaced by a hysterically relieved laugh.

Amidst me declaring to my hubby that I was a crap mum (brought on by the fact I couldn't express enough milk so that I could get some sleep while my hubby could feed the baby with a bottle) and him declaring reassuring words to the contrary for the thousandth time that morning, I caught a glimpse of something that made everything OK. My tiny little human, sleeping with a big milky grin on her face.

Did she think I was a crap mum? Did she think she had been given the dud and wanted out? Yes, she may have been wishing I would keep my wailing to a minimum, but the rest she didn't care less about.

You see, despite the days that feel like hell to us and despite the feelings of guilt we have, these tiny humans of ours really couldn't give a rat's ass. To them we rock and they could not be happier with their tired and stressed human, who answers at their beck and call, no matter the time of day or night or the smell coming from their nappy. We can do no wrong in their eyes, so we need to start looking at ourselves through them. We are bloody legends who singlehandedly grew all their body parts and are now keeping them alive on a daily basis. Without us, there would be no them – meaning us mums are pretty bloody spectacular, no matter what the guilt trip that is currently trying to make us feel crap says.

So, let's all scream out together: 'Oi, mummy guilt, be on your way before me and my knackered mum self, kick your manipulative and evil arse into that pile of fermenting dirty nappies I still have not had time to dispose of or feel guilty about!'.

Amen to that, sisters!

CHAPTER 8

AFTER THE AFTER (BIRTH) PARTY – CELEBRATING OUR POST-BABY VAGINAS

So let's get it out on the table, shall we, your post-baby vagina. Not literally, obviously (it's not that type of book). But let's get the subject of post-baby vaginas out there and be brave enough to admit that, damn, our vaginas are bloody hardcore when it comes to the matter of surviving and recovering from pushing a tiny human into this world.

I'll get mine out first, shall I?

Here goes . . .

So, following the birth of my first tiny human, I can remember thinking, 'I want to be a sloth.'

Yes, you heard me correctly.

A sloth. Those weird furry things that live in the Amazon (I think) with the funny face and the crazy ass eyes.

Yes, I had made my mind up. And no, I didn't care that they are as ugly and as hairy as hell. I wanted to be a sloth because those bad boys moved slower than a dying slug being given his last rites.

And that type of speed is the exact speed I needed to be moving at right after pushing a tiny human out of my vagina. Move even a minuscule faster, and I felt as though my poor, post-baby vagina was going to burst into a screaming ball of flames, never to be the same again.

Yeah, you get the picture and will probably know exactly what I am talking about if you've pushed a tiny human out of your vagina and it now aches like hell on earth.

If your vagina was anything like mine was after having my first, I wanted either to divorce the lower part of my body or to learn to walk around on my hands. Any slight movement of anything south of my navel rendered me short of breath and short of speech – and losing my tiny mind with pain, screaming from the inside out.

Every jerk, every step, every time I sat down, every time I stood up, every feed, every reach, every goddam muscle was screaming surrender unless I took everything at the pace of yes, our friend the sloth! And I'm not talking a young, nubile, I can cross a one-metre branch in less than six hours specimen. I am talking an old granny of a sloth, who moves no faster than a tranquilised snail.

Oh YES! Sign me up for some of that *slower than the speed of a snail* action.

God, I have *NEVER* known pain like it. And the worst part of it all was that I wasn't prepared to even consider that I would be feeling such pain post-birth.

What was I thinking? And why the hell did I not even think about the pain factor post-baby and after stretching my vagina to ten times its usual size?

I blame all the limelight childbirth gets. Seriously, we need to start sharing the column inches dedicated to childbirth with our poor unsuspecting vaginas so we are all prepared for the prospect that some of us will discover that the body-shattering pain does not come to a glorious end once childbirth is done and dusted.

'Ooh, but if we did that, that would be scaremongering. That would be terrifying poor mums-to-be. They don't need to hear about the bad shit that can happen. They just need to remain positive. They don't need to know the truth!'

I am here to say: BULLSHIT

I was one of those new mums-to-be feeling positive about pregnancy, childbirth and becoming a mother. I had prepared for everything up to birth and listened to and believed wholeheartedly the popular line that every pregnant woman has heard at least a gazillion times before childbirth: 'Well, of course, it can be painful, but once you have that baby in your arms all of that will be forgotten.'

BULLSHIT! BULLSHIT!! UTTER BULLSHIT!!!

I am going to be straight with you, ladies. If you go through a birth experience that leaves you rocked and traumatised to your very core, if childbirth causes such damage down below that the recovery is a long and painful one, then the best thing you can be is to be prepared for it.

Finding out you can feel such pain post-birth, and realising that it can take more than popping a couple of Ibuprofen, soaking in a salt bath and doing some pelvic floor exercises to right the vagina wrongs of childbirth, is bloody horrendous and no mum should enter into it unprepared.

Now I know, as with a lot of things with motherhood, you never can truly 'get it' until you're actually living it. How-bloody-ever, a heads up would have been handy. In fact, it would have been life-saving.

To have known beforehand that I might have the overwhelming desire to chop off the lower part of my body/live on ice-packed sanitary pads/check myself into vagina rehab due to the level of pain, would have made life as a new mum a whole lot easier.

I would have been fully up to speed with how to make my life and my vagina as comfortable as possible. I would have known how to construct a sanitary pad ice pack. I would also have known you can actually buy them online, so I would have had a box of these on ice – just in case. Instead I was sent home, told to place ice cubes inside a flannel and pop a couple of painkillers!

I recall not even waddling but shuffling around, wincing in pain and sweating with pure exhaustion at the effort of moving as I tried to 'carry on as normal' after the birth of my eldest. I thought that the pain I was experiencing was normal. That every other mum was going through the same thing, and that I was the only one who couldn't handle it. The only one who, excuse the pun, was being a pussy about it. I'd convinced myself that the pain I was feeling was simply a byproduct of birth. I wanted to (and often did) cry at any sudden movement or jolt, so obviously I was just not as tough as other mums.

BULLSHIT!

What I didn't realise, because no one had told me – and the birth books, magazines and parenting blogs had neglected it as a topic – was that just as every mum's birth experience is different, so too is their recovery from it. Some women have the most amazing birth experience and recovery, feeling physically well pretty much straight after birth (I can vouch for this, because I had this experience with the birth of my second daughter). Some women have an horrendous experience and an agonising recovery that can leave them traumatised and never wanting to go through it again (I can also vouch for this because it was the case with the birth of my eldest).

If I had known all of this – if someone had told me about all the possible outcomes, the good, the bad and the downright traumatic – I would have been better prepared for my recovery.

Instead of trying to crack on as normal, whilst I tried desperately to get my premature baby to feed and latch on correctly; instead of forcing myself through the pain barrier as I reached over to do the night feeds; instead of forcing myself back into my maternity jeans and out for a walk with my new baby (because that's what all new mums should be doing with their little ones, right?) I would have taken proper care of myself. I would have asked for more help. I would have taken things easier and made sure people did not expect or ask too much of me. I would not have made myself feel like I just had to suck it up and get on with it as every other mum seemed to be doing. I would have expressed to my husband the level of pain I was in, though he would probably have had an inkling since I had shared all the other things

I had learnt from the books. I would have been kinder to myself. I would have shown my amazing body and my rock star of a vagina, which was now trying to recover, more respect.

I would have been prepared. I would therefore have had a better recovery. I've found so far that, when it comes to motherhood, preparing for the worst and hoping for the best works a treat.

It's so important to tell the truth about our experiences, no matter how scary. If we don't, the reality can turn out to be another scale of terrifying – and who needs that after becoming a mum?

It is particularly important to share the truth about the aftermath and effects of childbirth. Thousands of women every year are left traumatised by birth. They are at home, taking care of a newborn tiny human, feeling isolated and silent in suffering with their post-birth recovery.

What a difference it would make to our recovery and quality of life as new mums if we all had a post-birth plan (just like a birth plan) to consult. A plan detailing the possible outcomes and how best to take care of our minds and our bodies to help our physical and mental recovery following childbirth. Wouldn't the whole process be a whole lot easier, a whole lot kinder if this was considered normal? Instead, millions of women worldwide ask the same question: 'Why didn't anyone tell me?'.

For the sake of ourselves, our post-baby vaginas and our physical and mental wellbeing, we need to prepare ourselves for the good, the bad and the ugly of motherhood – and aftercare should be at the top of our agenda.

Trout Pout – no, not the lips on your face
(An ode to sore and swollen vaginas everywhere)

Out of respect for post-baby vaginas and their owners worldwide, I give you my little rhyme to help you laugh in the face of the fear we all face at the thought of laying eyes on our post baby vaginas for the first time. (By the way, my 'first time' face to face with my post-baby

vagina was in a mirror handed to me by my French midwife in front
of my husband forty-eight hours after pushing a tiny human out of it.)

Mirror, mirror between my thighs,
You've sure given this mum one nasty surprise.

I expected things were not going to look 'cosy',
That my lady garden may no longer be rosy,

But for fuck's sake, no one prepared me for this!
How will I have sex again, let alone take a piss?!

You cannot deny the scary, eye-watering sight,
When forced to look at your vagina in stark daylight.

It will 'make you feel better' the midwife said,
But instead it just filled me with horror and dread.

Although never known as that pretty before,
It's now less supermodel, more stitches and gore.

You see, post-baby bits are never spoken about,
So I was shocked that my vag had a trout pout,

Please, Mother Nature, give me a damn break,
And restore me to normal if I must procreate.

In the meantime, I'll sit on ice packs galore,
And pray my bits don't drop out on the floor!

GETTING INTO THE GROOVE OF MOTHERHOOD

Writing that subtitle has just made me laugh out loud as it is only now, five years into being a mum of two, that I actually feel I am kind of in my groove and getting more confident than I ever have been about motherhood. However, during the early days of motherhood I wanted desperately to feel that I was in my groove straightaway. I wanted to feel 100 per cent confident in what I was doing immediately. I wish someone had told me that I wasn't supposed to know what I was doing and that the only groove I needed to be in was one where wearing PJs all week and eating chocolate brownies for breakfast was fine as long as me and my baby were happy and healthy.

If I'm honest, things began to settle only after I came through the newborn stage (where everything seems to change hourly, probably because it does). We were now in a routine and I had more of an idea on what we were doing (kinda).

During this time, a big factor was my mental health. Trying to get a handle on new motherhood while also trying to get control of my maternal mental health was a struggle. I began to feel I could juggle the two only after I had started to take anti-depressants.

The tablets made me feel free of the fog through which I had been stumbling and lifted the depression that crushed me. They gave me the clarity that we mums are all getting a bit of a raw deal in terms of the image of motherhood we are sold whilst pregnant. It was the first time that I stopped and questioned all the books, the blogs and the magazines and asked where were the real accounts of being a mum? The ones that talked about how amazing it was but also how exhausting and overwhelming it can be too. Why had none of these media outlets included any information on maternal mental health and how to keep mentally strong?

These questions spurred me into action. Whilst Éva slept I started to write about my experiences of motherhood and my maternal mental health. I first shared my articles with my husband, who then convinced me to share them with some friends of mine who were also mums. They really enjoyed them and soon enough I had a reading group that had grown to forty mums – friends and mums I'd met via other friends – all reading my articles and sending me their feedback and sharing their own experiences. This reading group then turned into a blog and a secret Facebook group called 'The Baby Bible'. The blog and the Facebook group embodied the ethos of supporting all mums – no judgement. They provided a safe place offering support for mums wanting to talk about all areas of motherhood. Word got around, and it quickly went from forty mums offering feedback on my writing to more than four thousand mums sharing advice and nonjudgemental support. I was blown away to realise how many mums wanted an honest account of being a mum, and it made me understand that I was not the only one in need.

For the first time since being a mum, I felt like I was getting myself back on track. I was maintaining my mental health with anti-depressants, I'd started yoga again, and I had a close group of friends who had all become mums at the same time. I was writing every chance I got, and this provided a healthy outlet for the challenges I had faced. Having the support and the network of mums on The Baby Bible group was a godsend. I will never be able to thank enough the amazing mums in the group who have offered me so much love, support and laughs over the last few years and who are still doing so today. I consider you all friends and hope that one day I get to meet you all over a glass of fizzy wine.

CHAPTER 9

GOING FROM ONE TO TWO

Éva was around ten months old when we had the chat about having a second child.

I'd always wanted to have our children close together, and as I was heading towards my late thirties I didn't want to leave it too long before trying for a second. I was weighing up not just the normal concerns about trying for a second, but also the concerns of a mum with a history of maternal mental health challenges. So Jamie and I discussed in depth about whether it was safe to have another. When should we start trying? How long should we wait? And would my illness come back? Looking back now it is terrifying to acknowledge that our lack of awareness of the illness meant we didn't realise the illness had not gone away. Despite me feeling more well than I had since having Éva, I was still not out of the woods.

We didn't have access to any advice on having a second baby after suffering with PND, there were no support groups and not really anyone we could speak to about it since we didn't know anyone else who had been through it. I remember raising our concerns with our doctor, who said that getting pregnant again should be 'fine'. Just because I suffered with PND the first time did not mean I would do so a second time. (My postpartum psychosis, which you'll find out more about later, was still undiagnosed at this point.) The only warning was that I had to start coming off my anti-depressants before we started trying. So this is what I did.

We started trying for baby number two with the blind naivety that all would be fine and that – in the words of my doctor – 'having another baby would probably help sort out and rebalance my hormones'. A month later, I was pregnant. Éva was eleven months old, I was off my medication, and according to both the pregnancy test and the size of my boobs (enormous) we were having another baby. We were both bowled over by how quick it had happened, but also felt excited that after the hell we had been through over the last several months things were looking up. As a family, we were getting back on track, fulfilling our dream of having another baby, a sister or brother for Éva.

MY SECOND PREGNANCY – I NEVER EXPECTED TO FEEL LIKE THIS WHEN I WAS EXPECTING.

With the beauty of hindsight, and now that I am no longer suffering from a mental illness (which always helps), I can't believe I was surprised to feel the way I did when I was pregnant with our second baby. I had battled two maternal mental illnesses for eleven months (albeit one of them undiagnosed), and had been taking a course of anti-depressants. Despite the doctor having told me it should all be OK, today, with my now well and rational mind, I can't quite understand why I didn't question him. I know how ridiculous – and dangerous – this must sound to you reading it. I know you must be wondering, 'What the hell were they thinking? Of course it was too soon! Why could they not see that? And why was the doctor saying it was fine?'

I know you are asking all of this, because I am too. And you know what? I don't have an answer for you. I really don't. Believe me, I am sitting here now shaking my head and racking my brain for an answer. However, all I have is the truth that I wanted another baby and that I didn't want the illness to steal this from me; it had already taken too much. I was ill and neither my husband nor I had any real understanding of what we were facing, of what the illness was. We trusted the doctor and thought it was all going to be OK. Couple this with the fact that the medication had made me feel like my old self again and we both thought that I had come through the illness and were ready to start getting on with the rest of our lives. We were wrong. So very wrong.

PREGNANCY AND PND – 'PLEASE DON'T MAKE ME GO THROUGH THIS AGAIN'

This was what I asked – no, begged my husband to promise me. I remember the moment with such clarity and pain that just seeing the words typed out before me takes me straight back: five months pregnant, ill on bed rest and consumed with guilt for not being able to take care of my toddler properly.

From the word go, my second pregnancy had been a difficult one. I fell pregnant when I was feeling well and convinced that I had conquered my postnatal depression. Little did I know that my battle had only just begun – and that it was about to get a whole lot harder before I was anywhere close to being better.

You see, despite trying to deny it during the early months, putting my lack of energy, fatigue and low moods down to morning sickness and the difficulty of the first twelve weeks, there was now no denying that the illness I thought I had overcome had in fact returned. Before that second pregnancy, I had assumed that if I got ill a second time I would at least have the assurance of being forearmed, as the motto has it. Unfortunately, it didn't quite play out this way for me.

And why should it have done, I guess you could ask. Anyone with any sense would have realised that having suffered from a mental illness means that I was more prone to it returning – particularly after allowing myself just eleven months not only to adapt to motherhood but to recognise a mental illness and try to overcome it. However, at the time, the thought never even crossed my mind. I never thought: Hey, why not wait, you've been through enough. Oh no, after what I'd been through already in the battle against PND and given all the things it had stolen from me and how it had held me back, I was determined that it was not also going to rob me of my dream of having more children – no matter what the cost, to myself or my health. Today, I realise that this was incredibly naïve and just plain bloody dangerous.

However, this was the situation I was in, these were the cards I'd been dealt. Now my only option was to keep going and hope that I came out the other side with a healthy baby and a healthy mind. Yet at that moment, when I found myself (yet again) losing my grip on my mental health and holding on to my husband for dear life, I couldn't even begin to imagine how I was going to get through the next few months without something awful happening to me.

I'd started suffering both physically and mentally from quite early on in the pregnancy. However, when I was told I was having early contractions at sixteen weeks and that my blood pressure was so low I could no longer drive, I knew I was going to have to batten down the hatches.

It was heartbreaking not to be able to answer all the needs of my energetic toddler. Every time I picked her up and carried her around as she requested, the familiar tightening of contractions would resume and I'd have to put her back down. She would look at me forlornly, upset that mummy would not hold her. And as she had been born prematurely, I knew the chances of this new little baby turning up early were stacked up high. So, ensued months of me feeling racked with guilt that I was neglecting my toddler and being a bad mum coupled with the stomach–churning panic that if I didn't take it easy, I would bring on the early birth of my new baby. The burden of these two situations was at times too much to bear.

I had enjoyed every moment of my first pregnancy (once I'd got through the morning sickness phase). I'd been active, clearheaded and more content in myself than ever before. I was blooming and really enjoyed planning for the future of our little family.

My second pregnancy was the polar opposite. I was lethargic to the point that it was impossible to get out of bed – or even to stay awake some days. The feeling of contentment and peace I felt during my first pregnancy was now replaced by panic and sickening anxiety. And my mood was so low and debilitating that everyday felt as though I was walking through tar and not getting anywhere. I became insular, being scared to leave the house, and the thought of get-togethers with friends made me want to flee the country. I had such a self-loathing that I told my husband on numerous occasions to leave me, adding that I wouldn't blame him if he did. Today, remembering that scene, when I was six months pregnant and full of baby and despair, I don't even recognise the person I had become.

Throughout my pregnancy my biggest fear was: What if this is now who I am? What if the illness has got such a grip on me that it will still be here, stronger than ever, once the baby arrives? How on earth am I going to be able to take care of a toddler and a newborn if I am ill?

I felt ugly inside and out, was riddled with self-doubt, anxiety and anger. I knew that if I didn't get help, things were going to become impossible for me to carry on. This was when I decided to go for counselling for the first time. I needed to get a grip on my mind for the sake of my husband, my daughter and the new baby I was about to bring into the world.

Talking therapy helped me immensely. It provided a safe place where I could unburden even the craziest and darkest of thoughts and not be judged. It allowed me to vocalise all the thoughts and feelings berating my mind, keeping me awake for hours on end. The panic in the pit of my stomach and the barrage of guilt, anxieties and self-doubt running through my brain made me unable to sleep. I thought I'd never be able to sleep again.

I walked out of my first session feeling a little bit lighter, a little bit freer, a little bit more in control. It gave me a taste of the promise that I would not always feel this way, that there was a way out – no matter how long it took to get there.

My husband also noticed a difference in me – and in us – after attending the sessions. They started out as twice-weekly and by the end of the pregnancy I was attending once a week, with the option to go more frequently if I was having a particularly bad week.

Counselling was not a quick fix. It was like having a companion, who knew the darkest of my despairs and the most fretful of my anxieties and didn't judge me, but helped me work my way through them, helped me carry the burden until I was strong enough again. It also gave me a set of coping skills and techniques that I still call on today. It helped reinstall my confidence in my own abilities and helped quieten the shame I felt for being ill.

If you had told me before having children and before suffering with mental illness that I could feel this way whilst pregnant, I would not have believed you. Pregnancy to me, pre-mum, meant being gloriously blooming and content whilst I got gloriously big. It meant being happy to have swollen feet and a swollen belly. It meant having a purpose. It meant being grateful to the universe for allowing me the privilege to create and carry a life. I felt all these things whilst pregnant for the first time, so the shock of being able to feel such darkness during what should have been one of the happiest times of my life rocked me to my pregnant core. On my darkest of days, I feared that the darkness would pass onto and somehow harm the little life growing inside me.

It was an horrific time for me and my little family. We were marooned on an island of mental illness with no means of escape. This time is still a blur. A blur covered with a dark haze, which still makes me feel sick to my stomach when the enormity of what we went through hits me.

Perhaps it was a mix of the counselling sessions and the surge of hormones in the final trimester of my pregnancy, but something in my mind lifted. The dark shroud that had covered me for the past seven months shifted and started to let in some glorious light. I found

I could breathe easier, with my breaths no longer as constricted by panic, and the thought 'How am I going to get through today?' did not hit me each time I awoke.

The relief of this respite from the illness was overwhelming. I was fearful to trust it, but despite being physically uncomfortable and in pain from contractions, I did feel mentally well for the first time since becoming pregnant.

My naivety about the power of this illness had gone, and I had been through too much to believe that the illness had left me forever. However, this window of sunshine gave me hope that it was possible to feel well again amidst the chaos and destruction of the illness.

So, if you are currently pregnant and the experience is anything but wonderful, I do hope that sharing my experiences with you will give you strength and reassurance that you are not on your own. That other mums and mums-to-be are also going through what you are. Most importantly, I hope it gives you hope. Hope that despite the battle ahead, there is a way forward to you being well again and enjoying being a mummy – something you deserve!

CHILDBIRTH TAKE TWO – 'I'LL HAVE ANOTHER ONE TOMORROW'

In comparison to my first, my second birth felt like something scripted by Mary Poppins. I can actually say, hand on heart, that I enjoyed the experience. Yes, I know I used to stare in bewildered wonder at mums who told me this. Following the birth of my eldest, I didn't think it was possible to have a positive word to say about childbirth and felt that anyone who said they'd had a good experience was part of some cruel childbirth conspiracy.

Turns out I was wrong. Eighteen months after my first harrowing experience of childbirth, I was back in the labour room having a completely different experience. Thank God! Following the harrowing experience of my first birth and the horror of postnatal depression that followed me out of that labour room, I know that a similar experience would quite simply have meant the end of me. There would have been no coming back from the edge of that despair for a second time. My mind was just not healed enough or strong enough to fend off those demons again.

I will, therefore, be forever grateful for the positive experience of giving birth to my second tiny human. The positive warmth it bestowed upon me gave me something reassuring to hold onto when things started to get tough. However, like all birth stories there was still a twist in the tale: the labour itself was pretty textbook, but the run-up to the birth and what followed ensured it was still laced with drama.

It all started on a gloriously sunny day in July. After weeks of being on house arrest again, since I had been having contractions from around sixteen weeks, I was climbing the walls and desperate to get out of the house. I was thirty-four weeks pregnant, had already gone through a couple of scares at around thirty-two weeks (starting to sound familiar?) and had been told not to walk too far, not to pick up our toddler – and to take it as easy as possible (not easy to do with an eighteen-month-old running around!). I was fed up, hot, and desperate for an ice cream and some scenery that didn't involve the four vanilla walls of our home.

So I convinced the hubby that it would be a great idea to get us all out of the house for an ice cream. He took a lot of persuading as he was worried that I should be resting, but after promising him that I wouldn't walk anywhere and that I would tell him the moment I felt tired, he agreed. So we all got into the car and set off. About three minutes into the journey, things didn't feel right; I was getting the familiar tightening across my bump and sharp pains in my stomach. Dammit, I knew what this was.

My hubby had noticed I'd gone quiet (something I do when con-templating life-changing events or the potential of unspeakable pain) and asked me what was up. I tried to sound nonchalant, explaining that

I was in some discomfort, but at the mere whisper, the hubby swung the car off the highway and drove us all straight to the hospital. This time, it was only a short drive away; we'd moved house down the mountain several months earlier. By the time we'd parked, though, and got Éva out of the car and us all into the maternity ward, these tightening pains had advanced to sharp pains and I was finding it hard to speak.

All three of us and bump were taken up to the maternity ward so I could be monitored, whilst Jamie called our best friends to come and collect Éva; the nurses had confirmed that yes, I was having labour contractions and yes, the baby was on its way. It seemed that both of our tiny humans were in a rush to get into this world and no amount of mummy taking it easy was going to deter them. Once again, bang on the thirty-four week mark, our second tiny human was about to make an appearance.

Despite again being six weeks early and despite me not having had the steroid injection this time around, the doctors reassured us that it was perfectly safe to deliver her at this stage of the pregnancy, and the whole team of midwives and doctors took the very best care of me.

The healthcare team looking after me knew all about my maternal mental health history and that my first experience of childbirth had played a key part in my being unwell. They therefore assured me at every point that they were going to take the best care of me and ensure my experience was as good and as calm as possible – and nothing like my first experience.

My personal history was even known by the anaesthetist, who spoke to me in English (to help my addled, Brummie French brain). He said he knew all about my first experience with the failed epidural and wanted to assure me that this would not happen on his watch. I was even given my epidural when I was just three centimetres dilated because the midwives were aware of how fast I gave birth the first time and wanted me to be as ready and as calm as possible.

I honestly don't think I could have dreamt up or imagined a more calm and wonderful experience – words I never thought could possibly be associated with childbirth.

The birth was textbook, and went without a hitch. It took around seven pushes and she was here. Despite the easy and calm delivery, she was having trouble breathing on her own when she got here, so after a quick kiss on her lips, she was whisked away to the team of specialists, with my hubby shouting from the side room to keep me informed about what was happening.

Thanks to the epidural and because the whole experience had been a good one, I just wanted to get off the bed and be with her. In fact, I told the midwife this. After my first experience I had felt shellshocked, emotionally numb and in excruciating pain. This time around, I felt empowered, physically OK and just desperate to get off the bloody bed and get to my baby.

Unfortunately, she had been rushed up to neonatal. She was gone with my hubby and the doctors whilst I had an agonising wait for the go-ahead from the midwives to join them.

HAVING A PREMATURE BABY

Not having your baby where they should be (with you) for their first precious moments is quite simply heartbreaking (as any of you mums who have been through the same will know all too well). It was the most surreal feeling that this tiny person who had been part of me, sharing every moment with me for the last several months, was now in the world but not with me. I was not the one protecting her and taking care of her.

I quickly became a nightmare patient. I ended up telling the midwives in my best French that, if they'd done all they needed to do with me, then there was no way I was waiting around for the standard two-hour rest time post-baby, that I was getting off this labour bed and was going to see my baby. I remember swinging my still recovering-from-the-epidural legs around and trying to stand because I was so determined to get to her even if it meant walking on my numb legs. I think this showed them I was not going to take no for an answer, so they got me a wheelchair and wheeled me to the neonatal unit.

It was heartbreaking seeing her brand new and tiny little self, cocooned in her plastic incubator, surrounded by lots of scary-looking and -sounding machines. Lots of wires were attached to her teeny tiny chest, arms and head and she had what looked like a huge mask over her beautiful and delicate little face to help her breathe. I felt helpless and just distraught that this was how she was having to spend the first few hours of her brand-new life, surrounded by machines rather than being in her mummy's arms receiving reassuring cuddles and kisses.

It was around 6 a.m. at this point and the nurses told me that I needed to leave her and get some rest, reassuring me that as soon as I was awake I could come straight back down and be with her. This tipped me over the edge: I told them repeatedly that I was not leaving her and sobbed that I was not going anywhere. I'd been awake for thirty-six hours, had just given birth and all I wanted was to hold and look after my baby. I could not possibly leave her. What if something happened? What if she needed me? She surely knew I hadn't been with her so far and was already probably wondering where I was.

Both the staff and my hubby were amazing with me, telling me I needed to rest to be strong enough for her and reassuring me that I would see her the moment I had rested. I held onto this thought, that by going and getting rest I was doing what was best for her. That I could not be there for her unless I was well. That getting some much needed rest was taking care of my physical and mental wellbeing. From past experience I knew how vital this was. She needed me to be strong and together for her. So, still sobbing and distraught, I was wheeled back to my room and tucked up in bed.

Three hours later I was awake and determined to go and see my little girl as fast as my wheelchair wheels would get me there.

Seeing my daughter again for the first time, I felt a weird mix of emotions: love, fear, anxiety and *Wow, is that tiny human surrounded by*

all these tubes and funny beeping machines really mine? Does she know that
I'm her mummy? Does she know that, despite all this medical paraphernalia
keeping us apart, she is part of me? Does she know that the voice she hears
between the steady and regular puff of the breathing machine is her mummy's,
promising her the world, moon and stars? Does she know she's not alone?
That I'm right here with her and not going anywhere?

Seeing her properly for the first time and wondering if she knew she was not alone was one of the hardest things to deal with. That I was not able to spend the hours doing what the other mums and their newborns were doing – feeding, cuddling and breathing each other in; getting to know and feel every little movement, gurgle and tiny breath – was quite simply soul-destroying. I held onto her little hand and willed for her to know that the hand holding hers tentatively through the hole in the incubator was her mummy's, who was sending all these feelings through her fingertips along with a promise. That as soon as she was well enough and away from the tubes we would be making up tenfold for the moments we were missing currently.

When you have a premature baby cocooned away and on lots of different machines, it goes against every natural fibre in your body for your baby to be away from you. To not be able to hold them, cover them in kisses and do all the things you would be doing for them under normal circumstances.

You feel helpless and out on a limb as you hover around the incubator, trying to drink in every moment, every facial expression – and having to ask if it's OK to hold your baby's hand. It's heartbreaking to ask when you will be able to hold your baby for the first time, when they have been on this earth for twenty-four hours and you still haven't been able to hold them. It's all so weird and frustrating and at times awkward as you look longingly at the nurses, asking when things will be happening, when you will be able to have them with you and taking care of them all on your own. Your brain is telling you that of course your baby needs to be kept where they are to get strong and well, but your heart is longing with every beat to have them with you, back where they belong.

Going through this, not having my tiny human with me from the start, could have tipped me back over the edge of my illness. It could have triggered the start of a second battle, but somehow it didn't. Despite the anxiety and not being able to have her with me at all times, I felt extremely calm, strong and in control. I felt empowered and energised to keep as well and as strong as possible for this new little life. I made sure I spent as much time as I could next to her incubator, holding her hand, stroking her head and tiny toes – all so she knew that despite a plastic barrier between us there was nothing separating us.

I asked the midwife what their schedule was so I could be there for all her feeds, to help clean her and change her nappy. Through the days and nights I would set my alarm for every two to three hours, to express as much milk as I could for her. This all helped keep me sane. Although I was not yet able to do all the normal things for her as fully as I wanted to do, I knew that anything else I could be doing for her, I was.

Thankfully, this separation was only for a matter of days and when the midwife said the magical words I'd been longing to hear since giving birth to her – that yes, I could have her with me – I cried with happiness and hugged and kissed her repeatedly, overjoyed with the thought of being able to have her all to myself finally!

We stayed in hospital for around two weeks and I was able to stay in hospital with her in our own ensuite room (thanks to the French healthcare system). Pretty bloody amazing and I will be forever grateful for that time we had there. The midwives were on constant hand to help with breast-feeding and expressing milk as she was initially fed through a tube that went up her tiny nose and into her tiny tummy, with my breastmilk being syringed through. They then gave me one-on-one sessions to help me get to grips with breast-feeding. There was never any pressure to breast-feed or to stop and bottle-feed; it was all about what was best for me and her.

I think one of the things that really helped ward off any demons and any sense of guilt at not being able to have her with me initially, was the time we spent together, just me and her, during those weeks in hospital. After one of the midwives showed me how a body bandage makes a perfect sling device to carry a premature baby around in safely, thus enabling us to have that all-important skin-on-skin time, Isla-Mai and I went skin-on-skin at every chance possible; she snuggled safely in the bandage with her head popping out the top of my T-shirt. Our ritual evening promenade around the neonatal unit became a familiar sight to the midwives. We were together 24/7 and she was in my arms, next to me sleeping, or secure on my chest, held in place by my makeshift baby-carrying accessory.

These two weeks are some of my favourite of all time, and today I realise why. It was because I felt well and happy to be a mum. I was feeling all the emotions that I'd heard about when you become a new mum. I was experiencing what I should have experienced the first time around. I was relieved, happy and confident as a mum. I cannot put into words how thankful I was. I remember telling my husband how great and just how happy I was feeling. He looked at me with such heartbreaking relief and asked: 'Really?' I don't quite think he could quite get his head around it all, either. His wife, his best friend was back – and, like me, he didn't dare believe it.

I remember being so excited about having people come to visit us in hospital. I couldn't wait to show her off to people and celebrate how well she was doing. Things were how they should be when you have a baby. I was finally getting the experience other mums had been telling me about and I was hoping beyond hope that this really was my new norm. My new way of life. That my mind had been fixed – and what was currently holding it together so well wouldn't fail.

When I was asked about my birth experience this time round, rather than replying: 'Never again', I said: 'I would do it again tomorrow.'

CHAPTER 10

IN CHARGE OF TWO TINY HUMANS

JUGGLING TWO TINY HUMANS UNDER TWO

One of the things I struggled with the most being the new mum of two-under-two was the mind-warping logistics required to get anything done or go anywhere. Even if 'anything' meant only one of us dressed and 'going anywhere' meant sitting in the garden. S.E.R.I.O.U.S.L.Y. When I was stumbling my way through the early days, I would look at the clock one minute, and it would be 6 a.m. with us all sitting in front of CBeebies, dressed in PJs pebbledashed with porridge, and then the next minute it would be 3 p.m. and we'd now be half-dressed, still covered in porridge and still watching CBeebies, while I had no idea of how the hell it was that time already and we still hadn't managed to leave the sofa, let alone the house.

There' s no escaping that a baby and an eighteen-month-old toddler is a total headscrew at times, careering you from being overwhelmed with love and pride for these gorgeous two tiny humans to being just overwhelmed. Looking at the epic portion of motherhood now served up on your already brimming-over, running-everywhere plate.

With all of this in mind, I have put together a few sanity and survival tips that I stumbled across in my sleep-deprived, trying-to-keep-my-shit-together-and-the-kids-entertained state. So, from one knackered mother to another, here are my tips for juggling two tiny humans:

• Shit-hot organisation

As boring as this may sound – and bloody condescendingly obvious – I've found that if the three of you are going to have any chance of enjoying the day, then the type of shit-hot organisation that would do the military proud is vital! Vital, I tell you! Therefore, whatever it takes to ensure you are able to get them up and out the door the next morning, do it! Pack their lunches, pack the car, pack games for the park, pack toys for potential coffee stops, sleep in your clothes. As I said, WHATEVER it takes, get it done so all you have to worry about when you get up the next day is getting through the bedlam of breakfast and then you are out on the open road for a day filled with a load of tiny human fun to wear both you and the tiny humans right out.

• Don't be fooled

So if the bit above has you fooled that I am this supermum who lives her life with military precision – think again! I am so rubbish at getting organised, though I do occasionally, on a few days of the year, manage to get my dishevelled form and wild tiny humans out the house for a day filled with a year's worth of child-friendly, supermum activities. Which is a good job since it makes up for the other 363 days of the year when I can be found half-dressed, chasing naked bottoms around my house, screaming: 'Get your fingers out your bum and put your shoes on!' and 'If you don't let me get your nappy on, I'm calling Peppa'. It is an exhausting fight on every level and anyone who proclaims otherwise is a liar–liar–maternity-pants-on-fire or has a butler and a team of nannies.

So, go easy on yourself! If it's just too much of an exhausting task to get them out of the house, then sod it, have a PJ day, get out the colouring books, stick on a film and eat cake. There have been *sooo* many days where I have been in tears, beating myself with a discarded rusk and screaming I am a crap mum because the tiny humans have not been on the swings all week or we haven't made rockets out of discarded loo rolls at the local craft group.

GIVE YOURSELF A BREAK!

All your tiny humans need is to be with you, having cuddles and, preferably, eating cake. Therefore, let's lower the bar and just hang out, rather than hanging our already knackered selves out to dry.

• Snacks, snacks, snacks! Did you hear me? SNACKS!

NEVER and I repeat NEVER leave the house, the kitchen, the lounge without being fully armed with them. NEVER. I once made the fatal error of not packing anything of the snack variety and I almost lost a limb. Oh yes, my tiny human is not called the Biting Viking for no reason. I am now always sure to pack a chocolate finger – to reduce the risk of losing one of my own.

• Keep the little suckers contained

Baby carrier, double buggy, high chairs, car seats, gaffer tape, cardboard box. Whatever it is that can keep them both restrained, safe and not killing themselves or each other – buy in BULK. Oh yes, anything that allows you to get yourselves around the house/park/supermarket and cracking on with everyday life with at least one free hand and without the fear of God that they'll be running amok, hurting themselves or going missing was a win for me in my mum-of-two-under-two days.

• Get outta the house

Whatever it takes, whatever the time, get out of the house with them. Take them to a free open space and let those little supercharged tiny humans run wild and free, for as long as you can — and then some. Take their lunch or dinner with you, feed them out there, and then (singing/chatting/screaming 'LOOK Cinderella on a flying unicorn!' — whatever it takes to keep them from falling to sleep in the car), get them home, and into the house, into their PJs and into their beds. And relax, preferably with a glass of Pinot G.

• Bath them together

As soon as it's safe, get them bathing together. I know sometimes you would rather cut your arm off than go through bath time, but the way I look at it, it's another activity for them to do, one they can do together, one that (if they are anything like my splashing demons) burns off energy and makes them happy. And once they are old enough, you can watch them from the comfort of the loo whilst enjoying some me-time. Please tell me I'm not the only one that does bath and bubbles of the Prosecco variety? WIN-WIN.

• Buy them the same stuff

Buy them everything the same, identical, matching, THE SAME! I once scoffed, 'My tiny humans will be individuals in their own right, they will have toys that reflect their personality.' Fast forward to last Christmas and them trying to strangle each other with the lead of a yapping electronic puppy and shouting 'MINE, MINE, MINE!' and I vowed NEVER AGAIN!

Remember, everything is 'just a phase' and it too will pass

Like bad wind, teething, sleepless nights and hopefully post-baby piles, everything has its day and then before you know it, the time has passed and you can't even remember how exhausting it actually was. OK, so some of the brutal realities of juggling two tiny humans will stay with you forever (don't think I'll ever forget the pain of having a chunk taken out of my leg from my tiny human's jaws of steel and dribble), but even these memories will eventually be funny tales to tell in front of their future spouse. Every knackered mummy cloud, and all that. Also, I don't know about you, but despite the chaos, when I feel their two squidgy hands in mine or when we are all cuddled up under a mountain of grubby hands, dribble kisses and chocolate biscuits, all the rest is forgotten and the world feels right again (even if only for a few minutes).

The World Can Wait
(A Poem for My Babies)

The world can wait, the world can wait,
I've nowhere to be and no chance to be late,
No schedule to run to, no washer to load,
No important meeting, or clothes to fold,
No outing, no class and no play date.
You see, for once, darling, the world can wait.

If the world can turn, then the world can wait,
For I've something more precious than life on my plate,
Brighter than the universe and the Milky Way.
I no longer need the sun to mark the start of my day.
No rush, no hurry, no time-up to make,
You see, for once, darling, the world can wait.

The world can wait, the world can wait,
Stop all the clocks and hold time in its place,
Freeze that smile, that moment unplanned,
Keep those little fingers in the palm of my hand,
Cuddles, bath time and tiny dreams to make.
You see, for once, darling, the world can wait.

If the world can turn, then the world can wait,
Masters of our little universe, our destiny ours to create,
I choose to slow down and share mine with you,
To remember all the tiny things that you do,
Belly laughs and smiles that make my heart break.
You see, for once, darling, the world can wait.

The world can wait, the world can wait,
'Us time' is the new commodity I cannot waste,
You see, this precious gift won't always be mine,
Life will move on but, little darling, that's fine.

One day you won't turn and throw that gaze my way,
Your cry will no longer be what marks the start of my day,
Night-time feeds and day-long hugs will be no more,
No tiny toys or discarded food to clear from the floor,
No squidgy folds to behold and no hair to brush.
So hold on, world, I don't want to rush.

CHAPTER 11

POSTPARTUM PSYCHOSIS – THE DANGER OF THE UNKNOWN

I often talk about my PND and now, more often than not, I'm able to talk about my experiences without breaking down or without it triggering some of the deep-seated and inevitably hurtful memories that still have the power to knock the air out of my lungs and leave me emotionally exhausted. However, there is another element to what I went through with my mental health that is not as easy to think about. Nor is it easy to find the words to relive it in a way that others can understand, words that will not leave my family and friends reeling with guilt that they had no idea it was happening to me or viewing me in a different light because of it.

I've always wanted to write about my postpartum psychosis. I've always been passionate about sharing all of my experiences of mental health and being as honest as possible in order to give the illness and those who go through it a voice. However, I will be honest with you: even now, during the final edit of the book and two years after starting writing, I am struggling to find a place for this section. I'm struggling thinking about how you will perceive me after reading about it. I'm worried you will read it and judge me for choosing to have another baby and for not fully realising what the illness was or the danger I was in. I'm worried that I'm opening a box that is better left firmly locked and stored deep inside my mind.

However, therein lies one of the largest and most dangerous problems of this illness. Not only that it is an illness most people have never heard about, but that it silences its victims so completely that it cruelly enables the illness to remain undetected, creating an incredibly dangerous and vicious cycle.

So, with your help and patience, I'm going to break this vicious cycle, share my story and fully expose the demons that were once a part of my everyday life as a mum.

Here goes . . .

I will never forget the day postpartum psychosis barged its way into my life . . .

DEMONS

'Hun, there are demons flying around the house trying to kill Éva.' Not the usual words you expect to hear on a phonecall from your wife whilst you're out watching the footie with your mates. In fact, even as the words formed and came off my tongue, they felt so foreign, left so disgusting a taste in my mouth that I was already desperately wishing I could snatch them in mid-air and claw them back, before any damage was done. But it was too late – not just to stop the words from bringing my husband's world crashing down, but to bring my mind back from the edge it had been peering over, eyes half shut, for the past few months.

My illness had soaked through my brain matter, taken hold of my thoughts, my senses and my vision to the point that what I was seeing and feeling was incredibly and unquestionably real. Demons were surrounding our home. They were coming to get us. There was no way I could stop them. I was completely and utterly terrified.

I remember as my husband, shocked and also unable to comprehend the words his wife was saying, asked me, 'You what? What do you mean?'.

I replied, 'I know it sounds crazy, but I promise you there are demons flying around the house. I can see them, they are getting closer and are going to try and take Éva.'

It was only an hour after he had tucked his daughter up safely in bed. Now consumed with concern and disbelief, he said, 'I'm coming home!'.

'No, it's OK, we'll be OK as long as they can't get into the house.'

My husband arrived home ten minutes later to find me on my knees in the kitchen, clutching the kitchen sides, consumed by fear and confusion whilst our baby slept safely and soundly in her nursery.

This was my first psychotic episode. And despite it being petrifying and confusing, both my husband and I thought it was all part of PND, which I was already being treated for, so this was just another symptom, nothing that needed extra help. After all, I was already being treated. This was just par for the course, and I was going to have to ride them out along with all the other symptoms I was currently battling. I was taking anti-depressants and these would fix it eventually. I just needed to suck it up and carry on with it all.

This incident was my first taste of the illness and my first hallucination, but unfortunately not the last. It opened the door to a new darkness, and a place in my mind where I had never ventured before.

My next very real encounter with something so very unreal took place a week later. A three-foot, mint-blue demon was peering over my shoulder and baring his teeth at me as I filled the washing machine with tiny vests, socks and baby grows. It left me screaming out loud in fear – and then saw me laughing hysterically whilst crying with relief when I finally realised that it wasn't actually real.

These two encounters were my introduction to the world of postpartum psychosis. Unfortunately it was the introduction of a menacing new houseguest, who lived with me for the next three years.

THE DARK STRANGER

The first time I saw him, he was sitting on the sofa. I'd put Éva down for her afternoon nap, my hubby was out at work and I was alone in the house. I walked into the lounge to tidy up some discarded toys and muslins, and there he was. As casual as anything, sitting on the sofa, looking right at me. Watching me, filling my heart and stomach with an electrifying, debilitating fear that I could taste in my mouth and feel coursing through my veins. There was an intruder in the house and we were in unthinkable danger. It made my knees physically tremble and my blood run cold. He was sitting there, unseen and unheard by anyone else and telling me in no uncertain terms that he was here now. That he was after me and that my days were numbered. All said in words that only I could hear.

And so began my daily run-ins with what I came to call my Dark Stranger. He would creep around the house after me. He would turn up and take me by terrifying surprise wherever I found him: loitering in the kitchen, peering at me from the nursery door or standing behind me as I put Éva down in her cot for her nap. Confronting him in my head (which is how we used to converse), I would scream, 'Don't you dare come near her! Stay where you are!'. He would then scuttle off back along the sideboards down the hallway outside her nursery whilst I was left trying to catch the breath I didn't even know I had been holding and desperately trying to cling onto reality, for the sake of the precious bundle in my arms. I had to keep her safe no matter what. It became my daily mission to keep him away from her, whatever the cost or consequence to myself.

It is only now that I have more knowledge of the illness that I know I was suffering from an additional illness – one classed by the NHS as a serious mental illness requiring immediate and urgent medical help. In fact, the NHS website recommends that a woman who suffers a psychotic episode (such as seeing demons flying around the house) should be taken to hospital immediately for her own safety and for correct treatment. Instead I went back to taking care of my daughter.

It is a chilling and heart-stopping reality that any one of the episodes I suffered could have placed my daughter in danger, could have meant I made a decision that led to either myself or us both not being here any longer. So why the hell do us mums and mums-to-be not know more about this illness?

After several months of these encounters, my Dark Stranger became a permanent fixture. It's funny how something so terrifying can become so normal. How something so alien can become so familiar. My dark and menacing stranger became so regular, so part of my day-to-day existence, that as I walked through my day I was poised and prepared to see him. Even so, the very sight of him – no matter how normal and expected it became – still evoked a terror within me that was as potent and as poisonous as the first time we met.

He was always there, always watching me from the periphery of my life, whispering menacing, gut-wrenching threats and erasing me piece by piece. He was a constant presence following my initial diagnosis of PND and stayed with me for the long haul. (Oh yes, he was not a one night stand kind of a guy. Oh no, this evil bastard was a loyal son-of-a-bitch.) He was right there by my side throughout the first year of Éva's life, through my second pregnancy and right up to several months following the birth of my second little girl.

However, he did take a holiday once. There was a period of around four weeks following the birth of my second little girl where I felt well – and not just well but really well. Something had lifted, the veil of darkness and dread that masked every day had gone, though I didn't dare allow myself to start to believe his absence might be of the more permanent kind. (I'd grown accustomed to the cruel ways of the illness and knew the likliehood was that he would return.) For a while, though, he was nowhere to be seen – and, believe me, I looked hard. I searched for him high and low, visited all his usual hangouts and continued the search until I was convinced that for now he was no longer here. For the time being he was gone, and I was finally alone with my little family. I no longer had his unwanted company.

This window of respite came when I needed it the most. It was the break I needed. The reminder that this is how I could and should be feeling for the majority of the time. It allowed me to gather my hope and strength, and strengthened my resolve to fight the illness once it returned and the Dark Stranger installed himself into my life once more. This time, I would be ready to face it and fight the next, and hopefully final, battle that lay ahead. Looking back now, I can only question why I was not already armed with the knowledge of what this illness was and how I could fight it and overcome it.

Those weeks of respite were bliss. The two weeks before my second tiny human arrived, I spent feeling normal, and the happiest and most together I had felt throughout my pregnancy. It ensured that I felt calm when it came to her birth and assured that I could manage. It kept me glued together and hoping and praying that this glue would last.

THE SECOND BATTLE WITH MY MENTAL HEALTH

And it did for a while. It stayed, holding everything in place, during my final days in hospital after the birth of my second little girl. It even got me home and through the first two weeks at home, taking care of a toddler and a newborn whilst breast-feeding on demand. Unfortunately this glue was not the long-lasting, durable-until-the-end-of-time variety, and slowly but surely it started to wear thin. Within a few short months I was more broken than ever before, and there was nothing to keep me from falling apart.

My husband was the first one to notice. My slight edginess, irritability and anger couldn't be explained away or ignored any longer. I became extremely protective over my time with Isla-Mai, and would increasingly take myself off to feed in private even when I was at home with just my hubby and eldest daughter. Without even knowing it, I started to withdraw and became increasingly determined to carry on breast-feeding – even when I'd been up for three days straight, feeding on the hour, every hour. I felt I would let her down if I gave up, and because I had heard that breast-feeding can help prevent PND, I felt I couldn't dare give up as my illness would then return and I would be the one to blame.

This time around I was determined not to mess things up, not to get ill, not to ruin what should be the most magical of times – and determined to be a better mother. I was still in denial that anything was wrong and would half-heartedly agree with my hubby that I was not quite myself but insist I was OK, I was in control of things and yes, I would most definitely tell him if I thought I needed help. Was I a good actress or what!?!

However, time was soon called on the *Liv Kidding Herself She's OK Show*: my unwanted houseguest returned. Oh yes, seeing him sat there as bold as day on my sofa was the final nail in my wellness coffin. Just when I'd dared to think his absence meant he was gone forever rather than just on holiday, he turned up, sat on my sofa and followed me around the house with such a bellyful of vengeance that his sheer presence deflated me.

Like anyone after a good holiday, he returned rejuvenated and well rested, which meant he was back stronger than ever, running my mind and my nerve endings ragged, sharpening my tongue and senses, and leaving me with an overwhelming sense of defeat: he was here and my fate lay in his hands. I came to accept that this was now my life. This was now who I was. I believed that the real me was so far lost, so far buried under the destruction wreaked by this illness that there was no longer any hope of her return. This was now my life. My fight up and left me. I stopped caring. I stopped fighting. I simply gave in.

This total surrender felt good for a while. No longer to be fighting it. Just to be accepting. Not to have to try to keep summoning the energy to battle against such a powerful and controlling force. To hold my hands up and say, 'I'm done'.

All the way through my battles with postnatal depression and postpartum psychosis, one of the key things I remember in my more lucid moments is talking to my husband and asking what more I had to give? What more did I have to do to get through it? How much further could I go past rock bottom until I started the climb back out? How much longer did I have to keep fighting for? How much stronger did I have to be in order to finally be free of this illness that was ripping my life, my soul and my tiny, beautiful family to pieces in front of me, whilst I watched on, feeling helpless?

Once I accepted that my PND and postpartum psychosis were back, and back with a vengeance, I was so angry, ashamed and exhausted; I was totally spent. I'd had a taste, through my momentary respite from the illness, of what life should be like as a mum and what I should be experiencing. More acutely I knew not only what I was robbed of now but what my eldest daughter and I had missed out on. What the illness had taken from us. I remember thinking: How dare it? How dare it do this to me again? More importantly, how dare this illness rob my little girls of what should have been rightfully theirs – a happy and mentally well mummy to create nothing but positive memories. How dare this illness try to snatch this out of my little girls' tiny clutches? How dare it even make the slightest of shadows over their new and precious lives? ENOUGH WAS ENOUGH.

This was the turning point. This was me getting my fight back. These thoughts were what burst my bubble of acceptance, fired me to get back on the road to recovery. This was not the old me, but a glimmer of the new me; a mum–of–two who was, yes, mentally ill, but who was owning her illness and calling time on it. I was angry, determined and driven to protect my girls from it and to claim back the lives they deserved: a mummy 100 per cent well and kicking the arse out of this illness, forging memories to make them proud. One of these memories being their mum battling through and overcoming the most difficult struggles of her life – not just once but twice. How kick-ass is that?

I'd been here before, so I tried my hardest to use this as a tool in my armour rather than a chink. I had knowledge of the illness and how it affected me. I knew what lay ahead and as my husband often repeated to me, 'We have got through this once, we can do it again'.

When our new little girl was six weeks old, I restarted my counselling, twice weekly. I started doing all the things that had helped me the first time around, including little things such as opening the windows and breathing in some fresh air. Just this simple act of throwing open the windows in the house and taking a few deep breaths seemed to calm me and refocus my incredibly busy and over-anxious mind. I started going for short runs, which gave me a chance to try and burn off the anxiety that was fuelling me through each day. And on the days when things were just too much, I made sure I told my husband about it. I voiced my fears and at times just let myself be with the illness. Accepted it was one of those days, that it would pass and hopefully not be as acute the following day. I drew strength from the fact that there had been a light at the end of the tunnel once before. No matter how debilitating or hard it was at that time, I just needed to keep focused and keep putting one exhausted foot in front of the other and trust that I would eventually find my way out of the disorientating, terrifying and tricky maze of my mind.

GETTING WELL AGAIN – COMING OUT THE OTHER SIDE

Sometimes to bring about drastic change you need to take drastic action. For us, this came when Isla-Mai was twelve weeks old. As a family we were back in the grip of the illness. Yes, I was getting regular counselling, but I felt more lost and alone than ever before.

My dark and menacing houseguest had been away, and just as I had used this time to regroup and grow in strength, so had he. He knew his victim inside out, had studied her for months, knew her trigger points – and he came back armed with claws more potent and gripping than ever before.

During this time I felt like a tiny sailing boat cast adrift in a ferociously violent sea of blackness, being bashed and battered senseless by waves that were gaining in strength with each strike. This tiny boat contained my life and my mind, and I felt as though my hands were trying to grip the edges and keep it upright, afloat and balanced. However, no matter how hard I gripped or how much resolve I summoned, another wave of darkness would come crashing down on top of me, sinking me further back into that boat adrift in the bleak and unforgiving waters, and threatening to send me plummeting into the icy depths, to be lost forever.

Pretty dramatic words, I know, but God, the despair I felt was tangible! It seeped into everything. My days looking after the girls and going through the motions of being a normal mum of two were quite simply blighted by crippling anxiety, which was now such a part of me that to be without it would have felt abnormal. An overwhelming, deep sense of dread and fear had my nervous system working on overtime, to the point that when people touched or brushed past me my skin would tingle with pain. I stopped sleeping. My newborn lay snoring away next to me and I just lay there awake and distraught, demons running around my mind and filling it with constant chatter. I found myself shaking my head violently throughout the night to try and silence them.

I had ventured deeper into the illness in a shorter amount of time, and trying to acclimatise myself to these new conditions left me feeling fearful and powerless. The answer to my wretchedness and the thing that gave me something solid to hold onto and remain focused was the thought of my family.

We had lived in France for six years, first as a couple and then as a new family. We'd got married there, had fantastic friends there, had our two children there, and this is where we'd battled the illness. We'd been through a lot with this glorious country, a breathtaking and beautiful backdrop to some of the darkest and ugliest times of our lives. However, the one thing I didn't have was my immediate family on hand for that much-needed and invaluable support, not to mention general shared history, which makes life so much easier.

Apart from the times I'd been ill, we had been gloriously happy in France. That we missed seeing family regularly was balanced by living and working in a beautiful place, one that was only a short plane journey back to the UK and my family. However, in the midst of my illness returning, my cousin and his wife hosted their wedding on Lake Annecy, just down the road from where we were living at the time. It meant a week filled with festivities surrounded by close family members. It was the first time since moving to France that I had close family just a stone's throw away and the effect of this stayed with me long after all the wedding guests and members of my family returned home.

Their leaving left a void that made me feel so empty. Despite having everything – an amazing hubby, two beautiful and healthy little girls and living in a beautiful place – something huge was missing from my life. Without it I had no idea how I was ever going to find my way back. For weeks after the wedding I would find myself driving the girls and myself back to the wedding venue and the hotel where everyone had been staying. I would take the long route home, driving the opposite way around the lake, just so I could drive past these places where my family had been and which now held such dear memories of family. I felt such a longing that some days driving past these venues would be the only thing able to lift my spirits. To pierce the darkness.

Now I realise I was driven by the thought of what it would feel like to feel at home again. To have help and to have the support we so desperately needed despite our desperate denial. It took a delayed baby passport application and my husband leaving the girls and myself to go back to the UK for a friend's wedding to make me finally face up to what we needed to do to break the vicious cycle of the illness and drag myself back from the brink.

'I think we need to move back to England' were the unexpected words my husband returned home to from his trip to the UK.

It was an inevitable but difficult and sad conversation – almost like we were giving up on us being able to get through it all on our own. Now, however, we both agree it was the best thing we ever did to get me well again, and as much as it pained my husband to leave the life he had known for eighteen years – a country he considers his home and friends he considers his family – we both agree that we would do it again in a heartbeat as it meant me being well again. So, six weeks later, we moved back and close to my family. I'd always thought my husband was a special human being, but after weathering this illness with him, watching him struggle watching me, and seeing him give up everything he wanted out of life for us as a family, I know that he is a truly exceptional man and one I would have not survived this battle without. Thank you, Jamie, a million, trillion times, thank you! Thank you for not giving up on me. Thank you for not giving up on us.

So there you have it, we moved back. And I'm not claiming this was a quick fix. That the moment my feet touched UK soil, my mind was mended. That all was well. I am not going to mislead you about the aftermath of the move (which we are still living through as I write) or the fact that Jamie was, and still is, pining after our old life. Nor am I going to deny that after reality sunk in and the months clicked by, resentment started to seep in. The ugliness of what we had been through, what we had both lost and given up started to take hold, and so began a new battle for survival. However, we had come so far together, we were not about to give up at the final hurdle.

FINALLY BEING FREE

Did the Dark Stranger come back to the UK with us? Well, he did drop by and pay a couple of terrifying visits during the first few months of me being back, but though he tried to make a permanent return, he has not been able to break through the border control my mind is now running.

It's funny (in a messed-up kind of way), he was a huge part of my illness and, therefore, my life. Since he visited me most days, I thought the moment he left me would be more monumental. That there would surely be a huge exit performance, one last devastating stab at his victim as he made his exit from this stage of my life. An exit worthy of his terrifying presence in my life for almost three years. But there was nothing. It was silent.

Just as quietly as he snuck into my life, so he departed. He slipped out of the door when I wasn't looking, and although he sometimes stops and stares in from beyond the garden gate, he does not venture down the path. For months after realising that he was no longer here, and as it started to sink in that he was not coming back, I would find myself looking for him, walking into the lounge and expecting to see him on the sofa. I've found myself doing this again lately, almost testing the boundaries of my mind, letting myself ask 'What if?'. But nothing – thankfully (a word that doesn't even come close to expressing how I feel).

I also can't pinpoint the moment when my PND left me. I remember one of my greatest wishes whilst I was ill was just to be able to wake up and think: 'Oh, it's Monday' rather than 'Oh God, what is today going to bring and how will I get through it?'. So much did I want to wake up and just be 'Oh, it's morning', I imagined that when I did so it would be a 'moment'. There would be a fanfare, we would throw a party. Truth be told, it must have come and gone without me even realising, thanks to being run ragged answering the noises and needs of my tiny humans, from being caught up in the whirlwind of life as a mum. And isn't that a bloody beautiful thing? That I was too busy, running around like a loon, feeling exhausted, torn in two, like I needed more hours and more hands, too busy feeling anything but depressed, that the moment it left went by without me noticing the exact time it left me.

It dawned on me, probably after a month or so of having these gloriously hectic and normal exhausted mornings, that I felt OK, that it had passed. I remember running to my hubby, all giddy and shouting, 'I'm OK!'. He looked at me like I was delusional (again) and then the words and their meaning struck home. 'I'm OK! Like, I feel REALLY OK, and I've actually felt like this for more than a while without realising it. I think it's all over'.

I promptly burst into smiles and tears. We hugged and held onto each other and just stared at one another. There was no need for words. We knew exactly what we were both feeling. In that moment of our life history with the illness, all the dark places where we had travelled together, all the ugliness and hurt flashed before us and brought us back to this moment. The start of the rest, that was yet to come. We were free.

The Illness – and what I went through personally and what we went through as a couple and as a family – will stay with us forever. Like witnesses to a tragic event, both my husband and I are changed forever because of it. We cannot unsee the things we have seen at the hands of this illness. We are no longer the people we were before. At times we have both thought that the final victim of the illness would be our marriage. We have bared our souls and our teeth at each other. We have been at our strongest and weakest. We have been at our ugliest and ultimately most beautiful.

I do sometimes wonder where we would be and how our life would look if it had not been visited by this illness. Would we now be a family of three, even four children? Would we be living in France still? What would I be doing? Would I even be writing, since my illness is something that made me start writing in the first place? Would we be happier? More content? Better off? Better even, less jaded and wounded?

It's hard to even let myself begin to imagine these 'what if?' scenarios. And even harder to question if I would go through it all again, knowing what I do now? Honestly? I feel the illness robbed me of irreplaceable moments with my little girls. I would give anything to be able to return to those moments and fill them to the brim with the emotions and joy that should have been there in abundance without effort or thought. I would do anything to regain the innocent and naïve optimism by which my husband and I lived before the illness put out its light.

However, it has also taught me some invaluable lessons that I would not now be without and which I feel weirdly and uncomfortably grateful for. It put me, my mind and our marriage on a crash course in survival. A course of fighting, teeth bared, knuckles stripped back, getting up and going time after time after time, fighting for the survival of my mind, my marriage, my family. I've been to the darkest places my mind could take me. I've realised and witnessed the power and complexity of my mind and what it can conjure up and make me believe. It has pulled back the mask we show to the world and revealed the grit and determination I can find when my back is truly against the wall.

It has shown me my weaknesses, my ugliest depths and my greatest fears. It has shown me the pure and potent ferociousness of the love I feel for my babies and the sacrifices I will make to protect them. It has shown me that in the face of our marriage vows – 'for better or for worse' – we have endured the 'worse' more fiercely and beautifully than even our 'better' times. It has shown we have chosen well. I am a survivor. We are survivors. We may be a little family, but we are mighty and we can get through anything together.

For this I am truly grateful.

Thanks to all that I have experienced, I am proud to be me. I am proud to be Jamie's wife and to be the mummy of our two amazing little girls. I'm proud of our story so far and, more importantly, proud that our story is not at its end.

IT'S NOT YOUR FAULT – A NOTE TO MY DAUGHTERS ON MY BATTLE WITH MY MENTAL HEALTH

One of my most heart-crushing and soul-destroying fears that quite literally sucks the breath from my lungs is the thought that one day in the future, when my tiny humans learn about my experiences, they might think that me getting ill was somehow their fault.

That I was ill because of them.

I'm even hating myself for putting these words and thoughts down on paper. For breathing life into these words and making the potential hurt a reality.

If you are reading this, somewhere in the future, darling girls, you listen to your mummy: No! NO! A BILLION times, NO!

My mind broke down for a while after having you both and I lost my way. However, I never once lost sight of my love for you both. I loved you then as I do now with every ounce of who I am, every fibre of my being and with every pulse of the blood that flows through me. If I had been shown a glimpse before I was pregnant of what was going to happen to me after having children, I would still have gone ahead. Nothing would have deterred me. Nothing – not even my own downfall – would have got in my way of having you two in my life.

My darling girls, you are my life force and quite simply my reason to be. You were my reason to be well. You were my reason to keep battling despite how much my demons were telling me to give up, that you would be better off without me. I survived not in spite of you but beacause of you.

So just you know this, my girly swirlies, you hold your heads high and your hearts full, be proud of your mummy for battling and kicking the ass of this illness. Believe in the importance of fighting stigma, for breaking down social and emotional barriers so we are all more brave and more free to talk about the subjects we usually box up and hide away from the world. To speak up on subjects we feel passionate about and always believe in ourselves.

Most importantly, please remember, above all else, the only thing you are responsible for when it comes to my illness is my surviving it.

Love you in the whole wide world

Mummy x

CALLING TIME ON MY OVARIES – WHY I'M NOT GOING TO HAVE THE THIRD BABY I'VE ALWAYS WANTED

I always thought we'd have three children and I'm slowly coming to terms with the fact that this is not a possibility. It's a choice that has been taken out of my hands. It's a choice that has been made, not because my body can no longer have children and not because we don't want another tiny human in our lives. Quite the opposite, in fact.

We have debated having a third baby over meals in restaurants, we've argued about it during road trips and we have cried about the loss of our dream of what our family would look like. We have ultimately weighed everything up and decided that our family will grow no more. It's so hard, though, to get my heart to catch up to where my mind is. As, if I am being honest, I still feel as though someone is missing. When I'm walking with my two beautiful and healthy little girls, I sometimes find myself looking for my third tiny human and I am stopped in my tracks realising they are not here yet and that this 'yet' is by the day ever more likely not going to happen. When we are all together, I look for our missing person, the last piece of the puzzle that is our tiny family and which will make our little unit finally complete.

Please, please don't think me ungrateful for what I already have – two beautiful, happy and healthy children – and please don't think I am being disrespectful to all the women out there who would do anything to be able to have one healthy child, let alone two or three. However, I had always believed in my very bones that I would be a mum of three tiny humans. It's not a certain quota of girls versus boys, it isn't a gender thing, a feeling that I have two girls, so the universe needs to grant me a boy. It is more than that. It is a deep-seated emotion and belief that our family has room for one more.

Jamie and I have spoken about it at great length and our conversations always end with us both reluctantly agreeing that we would not survive a third war with my mental health. The fact that it is this old enemy of mine that has determined we won't follow our original dream of having more children and has stolen this choice from us, is quite simply heartbreaking.

You see, I feel like there is a voice deep in my soul telling me, 'You're not done yet. There is still someone waiting to arrive.' These feelings, and this little voice inside me saying: 'Don't quit now', I keep silencing and have played down to my husband as his mind is quite made up. Mine, though, is not. Oh, of course I say the words, trying to convince myself that we cannot have any more children, and that to put our little family and myself through all of that again would be downright insane and totally irresponsible. However, there is always this other little seed of a thought, that maybe, just maybe it wouldn't come back again, or if it did, it wouldn't come back as ferocious and strong as before. This time I would be better prepared. I would seek advice before getting pregnant, put all the right measures in place, and attend regular counselling – all just to prepare myself mentally. All to make sure I was mentally fit and strong enough for whatever lay ahead. This time I would do all I could and more to prepare myself and my husband. I would do everything I would have done, should have done the first time around. I would go into it fully prepared, fully armed and ready.

But would this be enough?

I am reading this back to myself and think I sound like the most selfish woman on the planet. That the thought I would even consider risking the future of our family is just plain irresponsible. And that I should just stop being so bloody greedy and be happy with my wonderful lot. And I am happy, ridiculously so when I think about us and our two tiny humans. But I am also ridiculously defiant, and angry at this illness (my old enemy) for taking this choice away from me and leaving me instead with the question that will remain with me for the rest of my days: 'What if?'.

HOW EVERY MUM CAN HELP TO END THE STIGMA OF MATERNAL MENTAL HEALTH

Throughout my battles with my mental health, I have dealt with a variety of emotions, from the fiercest of anger and debilitating anxiety through to feeling nothing at all. As I've become stronger, so I have found my inner voice – and boy, is it demanding some answers. The person who has lain dormant, silenced by crippling anxiety and self-doubt, is now brushing herself down and bombarding me with a barrage of questions for which I hadn't realised I needed the answers until now. Questions, I now realise, myself and every mum suffering from this awful illness need answering, if we are ever to recover fully. If we are ever to be fully prepared for everything that motherhood can entail.

Questions ranging from the ones we hate to admit to for fear of sounding whiney and pathetic – Why me? What did I do to deserve this? – through to the ones that appear in your darkest of moments: How am I going to overcome this? Will it ever not be a part of my life? It is only now my battles with my mental health are behind me, that I'm asking: How did this happen to me? Why was postnatal depression not even on my radar? Why had I never heard of postpartum psychosis? Why was my maternal mental health not even a consideration? This has inevitably led me to the questions: How could I have been so ignorant? And why did I not place any importance on being mentally prepared for motherhood?

Herein lies the crux of the problem: the subject of maternal mental health is not on our radar. It is a subject we have only vaguely heard of in passing or touched upon briefly in mother-and-baby books. It is a subject we find too uncomfortable, too dark and too shameful to talk about. In our minds and in our culture, becoming a mother is a topic that should only be a positive one. A topic filled only with talk of baby names, growing bellies and hopes and dreams of the future. It is a subject we shouldn't tarnish with talk of anxiety, depression, self-harm and trauma.

As an expectant first-time mum, my mind and heart was filled with nothing but love and excitement for the tiny person growing inside me and a joy-filled anticipation for the amazing future we were going to have together. Was I wrong in thinking and feeling this? No. However, with the beauty of hindsight, I can see that I was not best armed for the reality of motherhood and all it had in store for me. Yes, I had a beautiful, healthy baby who I loved with every part of me, but I was also gifted postnatal depression and postpartum psychosis – for which I was underprepared due to my lack of awareness.

The fear and misconception surrounding the area of maternal mental health illnesses is leaving thousands of mums like myself not only unarmed and underprepared, thanks to a lack of knowledge of mental health illnesses in motherhood, but also feeling alone and isolated. We are terrified about what is happening to us, we don't understand why we are feeling the way we are and we are unaware of where to go for the right help and support. Unless this changes, how can we as women be fully prepared for motherhood? How can we as mums help ourselves, how can we help others without knowledge of these issues in the first place? One woman in five is diagnosed with a mental health issue following the birth of a child, but how can we recognise these issues in ourselves or in others if we don't know how they manifest? Most importantly, how can we arm ourselves against maternal mental health issues and empower ourselves to ask for help if the stigma associated with them means that we can't talk about them with our family, friends and health professionals?

The answer is: We can't.

What a truly terrifying acknowledgement this is. With thousands of women giving birth in the UK every year, it is shocking to realise that many of these women will be entering into motherhood with no knowledge of maternal mental health issues, and will then, unfortunately, become one of the one in ten diagnosed with one. Without the armour of knowledge, how are these women expected first to recognise they may have a problem and then to know where to turn to for help and support?

So who is responsible for putting maternal mental health on our agenda? I am a huge believer that more money needs to be spent and more resources need to be allocated to provide all mums with the support and care they need when they enter into motherhood, whether for the first or a repeat time. However, I am also a huge believer of the philosophy 'If you want a job doing properly, then do it yourself.' So I am going to be bold and stick my head above the parapet and say that the people who should be responsible for making all mums and mums to be aware of their maternal mental well being is, in fact, US.

Every mum who has suffered and overcome a maternal mental health illness. Every mum who is currently suffering. Every mum who has a friend or family member who has been a victim. Every mum who up until now was unaware of maternal mental health or the high probability of developing a problem in motherhood.

Every mum needs to start talking openly on the subject of mental health. Every mum needs to be brave enough to talk openly and honestly about their own experiences. Every mum needs to embrace the subject of mental health rather than sweep it under the proverbial carpet. Each and every one of us needs to arm ourselves and others with the knowledge of maternal mental health illnesses, how to recognise them and how to overcome them.

With every conversation we have, every article we write, every piece of information we read, every friend we support and every question we ask, we are one step closer to abolishing the stigma attached to it and ensuring there are no chinks in the armour we all need to survive the battle that is motherhood. By treating our maternal mental health as importantly as our physical health, we are doing all we can to ensure every mum is mentally fit for motherhood.

We need to change our mindset and reprogram our view of motherhood. Yes, becoming a mother is a true gift and our tiny humans are amazing. However, our view of motherhood, our expectations and portrayals of it, need to be better balanced and give a truer reflection of its realities without judgement. We as women need to feel empowered to talk about our experiences of motherhood, and the magical and the challenging, the ups and the downs should be given equal space and column inches.

As a mother of two daughters who will hopefully one day be lucky enough to go on to be mothers themselves, I feel it is my duty to bang the awareness drum of maternal mental health as loud and as clear as possible. My promise to myself, my daughters and every mum is to keep banging this drum until it penetrates the consciousness of society and every mum worldwide.

Who else fancies joining me in making some noise?

*If you would like to show your support for The Every Mum Movement I've set up and if you share the belief that Every Mum Deserves the Right to Enjoy Motherhood, you can find out more on how to join the movement on page 7.

CHAPTER 12

FEEDING YOUR TINY HUMAN

Why is it that every time we enter a conversation about how we choose to feed our tiny humans we feel as though we are entering shark-infested waters?

Why can't we all just agree to feed our tiny humans and get on with it? No discussion, no debate, no mud- slinging. All just safe and secure in our own choices, the most important thing being that we are actually feeding our tiny humans?

I have had a mixed bag of feeding experiences when it came to my two tiny humans, both overeager to get here and arriving six weeks early. Unfortunately, they hadn't given my boobs the heads–up, so to get them working and ready to feed was an uphill battle each time.

The first time was much harder than the second. At one point, I was crying with relief when I managed to express 2.5 ml of milk (a combined effort from both boobs); another time, I was left crying with despair after fruitlessly pumping for almost an hour, only to be told by the midwife that it wasn't working because in my exhausted state I'd put the machine on the wrong setting and she'd only just realised. If I hadn't felt so utterly forlorn, I swear I would have strangled both her and myself with the bloody tubes!

Apart from that one time, though, I did receive amazing support from the midwives when trying to breast-feed. There was no pressure only to breast-feed, and no pressure to stop and give my baby a bottle. I don't know whether this level of support was because both girls were born premature and so more time was spent trying to help and encourage me to breast-feed, or because we needed to make sure my tiny humans were feeding in whatever form that feeding took, meaning there was no pressure and no judgement since my milk hadn't come in properly.

The experiences with my two children were extremely different. After the birth of my eldest, I spent the first week of her life in shock. The birth had left me traumatised and I was in agony, not being able to walk more than a few paces at a time. If I'm being totally honest, I felt incredibly alone and lost – despite being in hospital surrounded by my hubby and a ward full of neonatal doctors and nurses. Somehow, I just couldn't find my bearings or manage to find my footing.

Everything felt alien and out of my control, and it seemed as though I was failing at everything. My baby had arrived earlier than she should have, after a birth I had not planned, and now that she was here I was not able to function as I wanted and as I had expected since I was in excruciating pain every time I picked her up. My milk hadn't come in yet, so I was not able even to fulfill the one job that I was supposed to be able to do – feed her!

Until I had my first tiny human, I had imagined breast-feeding would come naturally to me. (God knows why I had this notion!) I felt that, yes, it was going to be hard work but with a bit of perseverance it would all work out fine. It started off incredibly well, luring me into a false sense of mummyhood. My daughter, despite being premature, was a good size (5¼ pounds), had passed all the tests and needed no persuasion from me or the midwife when it came to breast-feeding : she latched on the moment she was placed on me, and stayed there for the next hour. However, following this first glorious moment where I thought that was it, we'd cracked it without even trying, things didn't carry on to plan. (My mum-of-two self is now saying: 'No shit, Sherlock!'.)

Despite first impressions, my milk just wasn't there yet properly and so followed hours of my boobs, and in particular my now incredibly sore nipples, being manhandled by any midwife going. This was accompanied by the relentless feeding and pumping schedule, trying to feed her from each boob for twelve minutes each (a random number, I know), which just exhausted my tiny human who should still have been cocooned inside me. This was then followed by bottle-feeding her the miniscule amount of milk I'd managed to produce at the last pump session and then topping her up with preemie formula (either by tube or bottle). Then I would place her back into her cot on wheels and as she slept I would begin the pumping sessions again, pumping for twenty minutes on each side. By the time I had squeezed out 5 ml from each boob and handed it to the midwife, I would then pace my way back slowly to our bed and lie there for around ten minutes before the whole two-hourly schedule started again. These feeding shifts were exhausting and made me feel like a failure: not only had my body let her down by not being able to keep her safe and where she belonged for the full nine months, but now after ejecting her from the only home she knew, it could not feed her the milk she needed to ensure she was strong and healthy enough for us to leave the hospital.

The nights sitting on our own in the brightly lit feeding room in the neonatal unit, trying to get her to latch on through the pain, to manoeuvre her into a position comfortable for both of us, to keep her awake so she had a full feed, were exhausting. I would sit there watching her feed from me but with no idea if she was even getting any milk or how much, and then feeling like a failure when I had to resort to a bottle and could produce only 3 ml of milk despite pumping for an hour. Exhausted, in pain and feeling lonely, watching this little person sleep (a little person who now miraculously belonged to me and who was my sole responsibility), I was overwhelmed and at times off kilter.

I desperately wanted breast-feeding to work. I felt like a fake mum when it didn't. And even worse when I returned home, and after trying to keep up the two-hour change–feed–bottle–pump schedule that was keeping me confined to the house, decided that I had to stop breast-feeding and move her over to formula.

Friends around me were breast-feeding exclusively, and the fact that I couldn't and had reached the point where I didn't want to try anymore made me feel less of a mum. To this day, I feel uncomfortable talking about how long I breastfed her for, feeling as though I let her down for managing to keep going for only six weeks.

However, one thing I do hold onto is the last time I breastfed her. I made sure it was a really lovely moment. Just her and me in the house, together on the big comfy armchair in her nursery. No noise. No distraction. Just the two of us, looking out of the window onto a crisp snowy day. This moment was magical. This moment I hold onto and will never forget. It's the memory I use as my armour against the negative memories of feeling I wasn't doing a good enough job during those first few weeks of her life.

Without knowing it, I was in a really precarious place after having Éva. My mental health was in need of support, and my inability to breast-feed easily helped to compound my fears that I was not a good enough mum. By the time my second tiny human came along, I was determined to do better at breast-feeding. I'd also read that mums who breastfed were less likely to get postnatal depression. This knowledge proved to be a double-edged sword for me. On one side I was intrigued to learn that it could help and desperate to try anything that would keep the Dark Stranger from my door. Once I began breast-feeding, I was then scared to stop, fearful that my illness would come back full throttle and it would be my own fault as I should have breastfed for longer.

Thankfully, the second time around, breast-feeding came easier to me. The birth had been easier. I could actually walk (bonus) and wasn't in excruciating pain every time I moved (double bonus). And despite her also coming six weeks early my milk came easier. I was more confident in my abilities and more relaxed about everything. It was in its simplest of terms, just easier.

Because she was early, she was initially fed through a tube that went up her tiny nose and into her tiny tummy. This gave her the breast milk I was able to express and was topped up with preemie formula if I'd not produced enough. This time around, though, when I could manage to get only 5 ml (despite pumping forever) I felt a huge sense of achievement and pride rather than the failure I'd felt like the first time around. I felt that I was doing all I could to get her strong and healthy, and knowing that she was getting even a few millilitres of my milk made me feel that I was being the best mum I could be. Now that I knew how hard breast-feeding can be and that having a preemie baby means producing milk is more difficult, this knowledge helped me to be less hard on myself and helped keep me mentally strong. As she was born early she needed help breathing for the first twenty-four hours and was kept in an incubator in a neonatal unit for the next forty-eight, which meant that for the first day and a half of her life I was unable to hold her or have her with me. The act of expressing every two hours became my way of being there for her until I could hold her in my arms and have her with me at all times. It was my way of being a mummy to her. So anything I could produce for her made me feel amazing.

We eventually got to the point where my boobs started to work, and by the time we left hospital she was breast-feeding every four hours. Of course, all of this went tits up as soon as we left hospital, with the lovely four-hourly routine going down to every hour or every time she cried. I felt determined that I would not be giving up – even after three full days of her feeding on the hour every hour, when my husband woke to find both her and me asleep on the sofa where we'd been since 2 a.m. and said: 'You need to stop breast-feeding, It's killing you.'

With a demonic roar, I growled back, 'I am NOT stopping and do not EVER ask me to do that again.'

He was only saying it out of concern, as he was so worried about me getting ill again. However, I was fiercely protective about my right to carry on. I loved the fact that I was doing something for her that no one else could. That I was the one keeping her alive, well and fed. After feeling like such a failure the first time around I was making up for that, paying my dues and proving that I was maternal and I was a good mum. I was no longer a let-down.

However, here is where the problems started.

Breast-feeding brought with it a plethora of emotions and feelings for me, ranging from feeling like Mother Nature, the life-giving queen of the universe one minute to a slummy mummy the next simply for fancying a glass of wine.

I also felt pangs of resentment and thoughts of: Oh my God, what more can I give? I want to put myself and what I want first again for once. I've spent the last several months giving up things I love, and now you're here I'm still the one giving things up. I just want to have a glass of wine and not feel like a terrible mum.

These thoughts were all juxtaposed with feeling like a selfish, abhorrent demon who didn't deserve to be a mother, let alone enjoy a glass of wine or a night out.

It's such a crazy ride of emotions, feeling almost superhuman as the life giver and provider of the only food your baby needs, all from your own body, to the guilty thoughts of wanting your body back, wanting a glass of wine, wanting to wear underwired bras and not wanting to smell of stale milk. Did these thoughts make me a bad mum? And why is it that we feel we can't talk about them?

I can remember sharing the physical challenges of breast-feeding, sore nipples, expressing and feed schedules openly with friends and family. However, when it came to the other emotions it stirred up in me – well, those I kept all to myself because they made me feel like I was a bad mum. I thought that if anyone else heard them they would think I was a bad mum too.

Looking back now that I am five years down the line of motherhood, I ask why. Why should we feel as though we can't air all our thoughts on the matter? That we can't talk about all the emotions that are being stirred up inside us without fear of being judged? Surely, if we did, we would be more prepared, feel less isolated and be kinder to ourselves. We would realise we are not bad mums, just normal ones going through normal emotions and thoughts. We would all be more mentally fit for motherhood.

With the benefit of the kind of mummy hindsight you get from being two years further on, I want to go back, give myself a huge hug, pour myself a large G & T and tell myself that I had already done enough. I'd already fulfilled my awesome mum quota by growing and then pushing a tiny human out into this world. I had already done enough by loving this new little stranger with such a ferocity that her needs now instinctively came before my own. I'd already done enough and proved I was a good enough mum simply by worrying that I was not.

That, in a nipple-shaped nutshell, really sums up the fierce emotions breast-feeding conjured up in me, which had me veering from wanting to give my all and breast-feed for as long as I could to wanting to run to a darkened room, take a nap and not have to worry about someone wanting yet another piece of me because surely I had already given enough.

God, it's a real head-fuck, isn't it?! I often wonder: Do other mums feel like this? Do mums who go on to breast-feed for a year or more ever have these feelings and what do they to get over them? Sometimes it makes me think that maybe I was just too selfish. And isn't that awful to think about yourself? As you can see, this is still something that plays on my mind to this day.

Isn't it crazy? That after you've spent the best part of a year dedicated to the wellbeing of someone else, after putting your body through childbirth, after worrying about every little thing and making sure your unborn tiny human's needs are all met over and above your own, that you still feel like you are a selfish and unfit mother if you dare to let your mind wander down the path of thinking what would be easier for you?

The legacy of breast-feeding for me is that I still have to fight the feeling of being judged on the length of time I fed both the girls. When asked how long I fed my eldest, I find myself answering one and a half months rather than six weeks because I think that sounds longer, and I'm always quick to add that she was premature and my milk hadn't come in, and that I had PND and my hormones were everywhere – all as a form of defence. But defence against what, I hear myself now ask? I guess defence in case the person asking the question will judge me for not being mum enough to do it for longer, will assume I didn't care enough to try for longer, to persevere. But thinking openly and honestly now, I think it's mainly defence against myself and the pressure I put on myself. I'd see all the posts on social media celebrating mummies getting their silver, golden or ruby boobies and think, 'God, did me and my six weeks even make it to tin?'.

I understand that breast-feeding is to be celebrated and that we can feel proud of ourselves for being able to do it and for the length of time we do it for, but I can't help but feel that this award system also adds an extra pressure and leaves other mums feeling like a bit of a letdown if they haven't managed to reach bronze, let alone gold boob status.

I'm going to throw it out there and say, Can't we all just get an award for feeding our tiny humans, regardless of how or how long? In fact, scrap that. Can't we just scrap the awards in general? I know I may be irritating the hell out of some of you now reading this; I can hear you shouting, 'Why shouldn't we be able to celebrate the length of time we breast-feed for?'.

I'm not saying you shouldn't. I am extremely proud – at least, I am trying to fight my breast-feeding demons to allow me to be proud – that I was able to breast-feed both my girls. I just want to stop the categorising and point system associated with it, so that 'Wow, I MANAGED TO BREAST-FEED FOR SIX WEEKS!' doesn't turn instead to 'Oh, I managed only six weeks and it was only combi feeding, and it wasn't exclusively my milk because we had to give her formula too.'

So how about we all agree to stop the labelling, the categorising and the judgement and be a bit easier on ourselves? Let's instead all just celebrate the fact we are feeding our tiny humans (by whatever methods we can) and what an amazing thing that is.

THE EVERY MUM GUIDE TO BREAST-FEEDING

I wrote the following article on breast-feeding after the birth of my eldest, and it received a phenomenal response on my blog from all mums – breast-feeding and bottle-feeding alike – so I thought you would enjoy reading it too.

There's no getting around the fact that the subject of breast-feeding gets us all into a bloody tizz. I admit it has the same effect on me. When I contemplated using it as a topic to write about, I felt my stomach tighten with anxiety, my head dip and my shoulders broaden in anticipation of having to defend myself against a potential backlash. Now, I'm not writing anything purposefully controversial or antagonising, yet the feeling of anxiety is there nonetheless. And isn't this the problem when it comes to talking about breast-feeding? That no matter what we dare write, think, say or do, when it comes to talking about breast-feeding we are always in danger of pissing somebody off (despite our best intentions)?

Like the majority of mums out there, I have had enough of treading on proverbial eggshells whenever the subject arises. Therefore I am raising my head and the subject above the social parapet for the sake of every mum who has had just about enough of the ridiculous breast versus bottle wars. Who like myself is done with the judgement and hysteria that accompanies the topics of breast-feeding in public, the age we decide to stop breast-feeding, the type of breast-feeding we decide on and if we decide against it. On behalf of every mum, I am daring to ask: Why are we so bothered about how another mum chooses to feed her child? And why is it such a political minefield?

I'm pretty confident that if I stopped any mum in the street and asked her thoughts on how another mum decides to feed her child, she would quite rightly tell me that she has enough on her plate worrying about how she feeds, rears and cares for her own tiny human to be bothered about the choices another mum makes. And as long as mum and baby are both healthy and happy, then surely that's all that matters.

So why, oh why, is it not this simple? Why do we instead feel so judged on our choices and like a failure if we are not doing what is perceived as the best choice when it comes to how we feed our baby? And, more importantly, why the hell can we not talk about it without the fear of backlash, contradiction and judgement? This has to stop!

For every mum out there who has faced judgement on how they choose to feed their tiny human, this no bullshit guide to breast-feeding is for you:

• Not every mum can breast-feed

Yes, we all have boobs, but this does not mean that each and every single pair will play ball and do 'what nature intended' just because we have a tiny human who needs feeding. Unfortunately, for a lot of mums out there desperate to breast-feed and desperate to do it well, it is not as straightforward as directing their newborn in the direction of the food supply. What is a beautiful bonding experience for some mums, one that they have found relatively straightforward, can be for others a frustrating and at times an extremely painful experience as they battle with a baby who cannot latch on, a milk supply that is unwilling and the guilt that, despite trying everything, they have to abandon their hopes of breast-feeding, leaving them feeling like they have let both themselves and their baby down. These mums should be celebrated for what they actually are – bloody troopers who tried their hardest to breast-feed even to the detriment of themselves. For all you mums with whom this resonates, you quite simply ROCK!

• Not every mum wants to breast-feed

Let's get the elephant in the room acknowledged once and for all by admitting that breast-feeding is not for everyone, and that the choice not to breast-feed for some women is down to the fact that they are unwilling. It is not for them and they would rather bottle-feed their baby. These women are not witches, they do not need to be hounded out of the local mother and baby groups and they certainly do not deserve to be judged. They are mums who are making the best decision for their situation. End of. Just because we are women and just because we become mothers, does not directly result in all of us wanting to breast-feed.

• You should feel proud of yourself for being able to breast-feed

Breast-feeding is challenging, magical and heartwarming. It can push us mums to the brink of despair on the bad days and to the edge of delirium on the good. It has the ability to make you feel like the worst mother in the world when things are not quite going to plan. And it has the ability to make you feel like the best mum on the planet when it's all going well. It is a journey of ups and downs and, most of all, a journey (no matter how long or short) that should make us all feel proud of and privileged to have been able to take part in.

• You should not feel guilty if you wanted to breast-feed but couldn't

As a mum who has been in this position, I do know, yes, that this is so much easier said than done. In fact, like most things in motherhood, it is nigh on impossible to stop the hell that is mummy guilt from bearing down upon us. HOWEVER, this does not mean the guilt is right or deserved. When it comes to mastering the art that is breast-feeding, there can at times be no rhyme or reason to explain why it doesn't work for us. Or why, despite our dogged determination and perseverance, it's still not working for us as easily as for other mums. We battle on through breast pumping, through sore, cracked and bleeding nipples, through mastitis, through problems with latching on, through problems with the amount of milk we are producing. We scour the forums and websites for advice, pleading to our health visitors and fellow mums for a solution on how to breast-feed and pacify our tiny human screaming to be fed. When, despite our best efforts it still does not work for us, we feel like failures and that our bodies have let us down. For all mums out there who have battled the challenges of breast-feeding and who may be feeling they have failed because they can't, please know that YOU HAVE NOT!

• It is not easy

Breast-feeding is an art to be mastered. It is a new skill for us mums to learn, and like any new skill it takes time, dedication and constant guidance – that you are using the right technique, sitting in the correct position, holding your baby in the best way – to ensure that you and your baby are having an enjoyable experience.

• You don't always get the right support or advice

Unfortunately, one of the most common complaints by mums when it comes to their breast-feeding journey is that they didn't receive enough support and advice, firstly on how to commence with breast-feeding and then on how to overcome any challenges. The lack of education around breast-feeding regarding how to start and maintain it for as long as is best for you and your baby needs to be addressed so every mum out there gets a healthy and supportive start to their journey and the much-needed advice and help throughout.

• It is not a competition

Before I had children and decided to breast-feed, I naively thought there were just two options when it came to feeding your baby – breast or bottle. It wasn't until I became a mum eager to breast-feed that I realised that there were a whole host of definitions under the term 'breast-feeding', and all had a different amount of kudos attached. All of a sudden we are being asked not just if we breast-feed but if we exclusively breast-feed or if we combination feed – and if we do give a bottle, is it a bottle of our expressed milk or formula? We are asked how long we have breastfed for and which method we chose and how long we plan to do it for. And all the time we are feeling that teeny bit more judged and worried about the reaction our answers may provoke. Again I come back to the question: As long as your little one is (a) being fed and (b) being fed, who really cares?

• You never feel like you've done enough. EVER

You could have breastfed your child until they were two, but there will still be a little voice in your head questioning whether you did it for long enough or for too long . . . You will feel like a phoney breast-feeder if you've used bottles as well as boob – even if those bottles were filled with your own milk. You will beat yourself up if you express milk so your partner can do a feed and you can get a few hours of much-needed sleep, or if, heaven forbid, you fancy a glass of wine. As mums, we are programmed to beat ourselves up regardless of how selfless we have been. Sounding familiar? Just remember you grew a whole tiny human, fingers, toes and the little mouth that you are now worrying about feeding. You are quite simply magnificent!

• We are ALL defensive when it comes to how we feed our babies

Hell, we are all defensive about all the choices we make regarding our tiny humans. They are the most precious things in the world to us. They are our gorgeous, chubby-legged superstars, for whom we would do anything. So each and everyone of us are going to come out fighting, teeth bared and tongues sharpened, if anyone dares to suggest that we are not doing right by them. So how about we just stop? How about, rather than passing judgement on whether a mum prefers bottle to boob or boob to bottle or on how long a mum chooses to breast-feed and by what method – how about we just don't? And instead just think to ourselves that mummy and baby are happy and that's all that matters. And, more importantly, make an effort not to be offended by all comments about breast-feeding.

• Your boobs. Your baby. Your choice

Whatever your decision, whatever journey you choose when it comes to breast-feeding and how you choose to feed your child, it's up to you. Anyone who dares judge can quite frankly 'Do one!'.

Ladies, we are all on the same team, breast-feeding and bottle-feeding mums alike. Therefore, all mothers battling the guilt of being unable to breast-feed. All mothers enjoying every minute of their breast-feeding journey. All mothers whose journey had to end before they were ready. And all mothers who chose to not begin the journey in the first place. Every Mum feeding their tiny humans (whether it be bottle or boob), I salute you. You are doing an amazing job – and don't let anyone else make you feel otherwise.

'Holy SHIT, Take a Look at My Tits'
(An ode to lactating boobs the world over)

Holy shit! take a look at my tits!
Their girth is as big as my head,
Bursting with milk and aching like hell,
I can no longer roll over in bed.

HOLY SHIT! Take a look at my tits!
I simply have no control,
No matter where or when, just one sound of a cry,
And this milk float is ready to roll.

HOLY SHIT! Take a look at my tits!
They're growing bigger by the hour,
Baby, you better be hungry and it better be now,
I'm dressed and don't want a milk shower.

HOLY SHIT! Take a look at my tits!
My partner is all full of lust,
Counting the hours, till he gets his fine hands,
On his wife's amazing new bust.

HOLY SHIT! Take a look at my tits!
My hubby is now full of fear,
An overamorous cuddle started a ginormous milk puddle,
So no longer will he come anywhere near.

HOLY SHIT! Take a look at my tits!
Please come closer and have a good stare,
They fed my babe well and did a great job,
What a wonderful and fabulous pair!

CHAPTER 13

THE EVERY MUM GUIDE TO WEANING

So, just when you've cracked the milk feeding schedule, the 'joyous' phase of weaning creeps up on you – otherwise fondly known as trying to force feed your tiny human spoonfuls of mush whilst feeling sick with panic that you are going to make them choke to death.

Oh yes, an overboiled, overmushed vegetable can have us dangling from the precipice of victory or disaster!

I was really looking forward to weaning. To seeing my tiny human's face light up with wonder at the palette-engaging delights of home-cooked food for the first time. Food that had been loving prepared by the fair and confident hands of her own mother, who watched on with joy and satisfaction as her tiny human wolfed down the lot and asked for more, despite not being able to speak yet. Oh yes, my food was going to be that good that it even performed the miracle of bringing speech to my six-month old, who, by the way, would also be expertly holding and sucking on a stick of organic asparagus for that all-important baby-led bloody weaning.

Fast forward to reality and there I was, sitting on the floor of my mum's kitchen, my tiny human sat in her Bumbo seat in between my legs, as I cracked open a jar of fruit purée and said a little prayer to keep her from choking on it. The whole momentous moment was captured on her daddy's phone. Her face was a picture and by the end of a couple of forced mouthfuls (whilst she gave me the 'What the hell are you doing?' eyes) most of the purple goop ended up spat out on her, me, the floor, the kitchen cupboards, walls and anything within a three-mile radius. And so our weaning journey began.

It made me feel excited that she was at the next big stage of her development and experiencing new things, but it also made me feel petrified and anxious once again. As with other tiny human milestones, I found myself trying to navigate us through a whole new ocean of unchartered waters, which raised yet another batch of anxious questions. How much should she be eating? What should I be feeding her? Are jar foods the creation of the devil? Should my freezer be filled to the brim with rows of homemade purées, all labelled and in cute matching Tupperware pots? (Please note I have NEVER owned matching Tupperware; I'm sure I buy them with matching lids, but as soon as they enter my home and the cupboard of doom, all hell breaks loose and those damn matching lids are never to be seen again.) How would this all affect her milk (something I now finally felt confident about)? What the hell was baby-led weaning? And once I'd found out what it was, dear God, how the hell am I going to let her put things in her mouth without the urge to panic she is choking and dialling 999?

I spent hours of my life (hours I cannot get back, I may add), puréeing mixes of different fruits and veggies. I even got suckered into buying a bloody Babycook machine, and then proceeded to poach chicken and mince. (If you ever want to know what a dead person feels like, I suggest overpoaching a strip of chicken in a Babycook.)

My freezer, once packed with gin- and vodka-infused ice cubes, was now packed to bursting with my melange of mush whilst the gin went warm on the kitchen side. Yes, my life was THIS rock and roll. My pièce de résistance, the crowning glory, golden moment of my weaning life was when I managed to kid myself I was Annabel Karmel and spent six hours – YES, you read right – SIX HOURS making small, beautifully formed and tiny human-friendly, well balanced, nutritional shepherd's pies. I felt like the Don! The Godfather of mush, wielding baby-feeding power with my Babycook.

As those perfectly formed bad boys came out the oven I could hear the chorus chanting: 'Watch out, ladies, there's a new mum on the block and she is killing it in the kitchen with her perfect shepherd's pie prowess.'

Who the hell was I kidding?

Certainly, not my tiny human, who took one look at my delicious pies and decided that the best place for them was not in her mouth or even on her spoon. Oh no, the best place for my deliciously, nutritious and beautifully formed pies, which had taken me six long hours to make, six longs hours that I was never getting back, was spat out on the floor and all over me in the perfect pebbledash splatter which only a tiny human can perfect.

I am proud to say that I handled the situation and this blatant insult to my culinary skills with grown-up patience and dignity. I most certainly did not leave my tiny human in her seat in the lounge sucking on a piece of cucumber, whilst I took the spat-out shepherd's pie back into the kitchen and sobbed my heart out to my hubby. No, that blubbing mess, reaching for the jar of purée I knew she would eat, was most definitely not me.

And so the games began, along with the ritual of spending too many hours of my life trying to make well balanced, nutritional and tasty tiny human food, for it only to be spat out hours later – at which point I'd reach for something, anything 'home-opened'. It's a ritual I know is common amongst all us mums and is happening across the world right now. And before you have time to blink or put a wash on, this ritual transforms itself into toddler teatime hell, with you STILL being covered head to toe in spat-out food and trying to disguise a carrot baton as a magical orange chip.

So let's make this whole weaning malarkey a load easier for us all, shall we? And really get to the crux of this winning weaning technique once and for all.

ALL THE THINGS I WISH SOMEONE HAD TOLD ME BEFORE I BOUGHT THE BABYCOOK:

OK. So, I'm going to be straight with you: writing about puréeing overcooked veggies is actually boring the hell out of me and since I don't want to peddle you anything other than entertainment because I know your time is short, let's instead cut to the chase.

So, for every mum out there currently pulling your hair out at how the hell to start weaning your baby without killing them, here are a few little nuggets of advice (not the chicken variety, though do keep these in mind as your surefire way to get them eating something – just don't tell Jamie Oliver).

1. You are not going to kill your tiny human.

2. You don't have to be Annabel Karmel or Ella's Kitchen or even be able to cook to be able to make tiny human-friendly meals.

3. It doesn't even matter if they even eat the bloody stuff you make them or not. For the first year, they are still getting their nutrient intake from their milk – SERIOUSLY! (Why did no one tell me this until she was over twelve months?)

4. How to make a main course: take a vegetable (say a carrot), peel that carrot, boil that bad boy and then blend the crap out of it with a hand blender. (Unlike my good self, you do not need to invest in a Babycook device, no matter how many mum reviews tell you that you NEED one in your life. You don't.) Pop that purée into a bowl, let it cool and feed it on up to your tiny human. Put the

rest of the mix into an ice cube tray, pop it in the freezer and, hey presto, you have a batch of weaning meals for the week.

5. How to make a dessert. Get a banana, get a fork, peel banana, mush it up and serve.

6. Cover yourself in a bin liner or take off all your clothes because you are going to get covered in regurgitated carrot. And that stuff is a biach to get out. Fact.

The End.
Bon appétit and all that jazz!

As mums, we all face a plethora of practical anxieties and hurdles to jump over with every new milestone our tiny human reaches. We provoke our exhausted minds with perfect images and tales of perfect mums handling these milestones in the perfect, shiny, perfect image of (you guessed it) perfection. All of which make us feel as though our own reality falls a bit short of the mark. Therefore, I am a BIG believer that we should say to hell with perfection and instead share the realities of getting through these milestones (weaning, crawling, walking, potty training) in all their hilarious, exhausting, and real glory. That way, we are sharing the anxieties of them, easing the burden and taking away the pressure. Reassuring us all instead with some much needed honesty and support and the laughs of solidarity, all of which help to keep every mum sane and mentally fit to deal with motherhood and its milestones.

CHAPTER 14

SNAPPING BACK INTO YOU, POST-BABY

One of the elements of motherhood that we do not prepare ourselves for beforehand is how we will feel about ourselves post-baby and how this new view of ourselves can effect every part of our lives, from our body image and body confidence to our career ambitions, our sense of style and sexuality. I never once paid any thought to how or if becoming a mum would change how I fitted into the world or how I would view myself in it as a mum. However, it has been something I've thought about a lot since becoming a mum of two, and still to this day I find myself asking the question: 'How do I be me after you?'.

I don't know about you, but ever since entering the world of motherhood, I feel like I've entered this special room that now contains my new life. It's a really lovely room, filled with some of my most favourite things and I share it with three of my most favourite people. It's a room that keeps me safe (well, safe-ish thanks to the discarded Mega Bloks) and where I have become to feel at my most comfortable. It is a room where I am in charge and a room where I am the key decision-maker.

There is a door on my room and though it is one that freely

opens, I do also, at times, feel like there is no way out. This room and everything in it is my new existence. I may still be able to see everything from my life before and everything that happens outside of this room, but sometimes I feel as though I am no longer a piece in the bigger picture puzzle of everyday life. I admit that I sometimes feel trapped. Immobilised in time. Caught in the net of motherhood with no idea if I'll ever swim free and independent once more.

When we enter the world of motherhood for the first time, we are joining a new club, filled with new members we have never met before, new challenges and skills we have to master, along with a whole new language. We find ourselves living in a new time zone; days and hours no longer look or function the same as before. We are on a totally different schedule to the rest of civilisation. We are aware that civilisation is happening around us, running simultaneously alongside us, but we are so encased in our motherhood bubble and living in our 'room' that we feel somehow separate.

This separation works for a while – and hell, is needed in those first months of establishing our new role as mum, beginning to learn about this new world we're in and the new tiny human we are in it with. Negotiating our way around the new challenges, we become masters of the new required skill set and proficient in the new language. However, once all this is done, once you are secure (ish) that you have bedded into your new role, how do you then make it back out into civilisation and bridge the gap between your old life, your new role and the current world at large?

It's bloody scary, I tell you.

I can remember pre-baby thinking that my life post-baby would be exactly the same, just with a new addition seamlessly slotted into it. However, after having a few months in my new role as mum, I found I was questioning everything. Should I return to my career? If so, when? What should I be wearing now I'm a mum? How should I now be acting? And how on earth will I slot back into the world at large that has continued to change and progress forward whilst I was sitting in my PJs, trying to get my head around feed schedules, bedtime routines and sleepless nights?

The world I knew had moved on and instead I had been frozen in time, cocooned in my little new mum bubble. My corner of the world had changed irreversibly, I had been through the most monumental moments and changes of my life, but the world at large hadn't stopped with me to take it in and had instead carried on regardless. How was I ever going to catch up with it or fit into it again?

Carving out a new piece in the universe for your new mum-shaped self is exhilarating, intimidating and downright scary as shit! Figuring out how you now fit into the world at large as a mum, and if that means figuring how to continue with your career? Wondering what your style is now, as it's been so long since you've been shopping for anything other than nappies and baby-gros. Asking how to behave as a mum – are we still allowed to go out, have one too many vinos, slur one too many words and still arrive home with our mummy crown intact and without social services or the mummy guilt police knocking on our door?

It's unavoidable the fact that motherhood changes you. It adds an extra ingredient to your true self and an additional strand to your makeup, changing your emotional DNA forever. I found that as well as making me feel confident in my abilities to keep my tiny humans alive, motherhood, filled me with a hell of a lot of insecurities, leaving me unsure of my footing in areas of my life through which I strode confidently pre-motherhood.

It may sound silly to some, but pre-motherhood High Street stores such as Zara, H&M and Topshop used to be my natural habitat, a place where I felt at home. They were my carefree nirvana. I loved spending hours (literally) browsing for nothing in particular that I needed; it was my favourite type of shopping. Throwing together sassy and 'on-the-money' outfits, I prided myself for having a bit of an eye for putting together pieces you wouldn't look twice at hanging on the rails but that, once in the changing rooms, would just work.

I loved it. It was one of my guilty pleasures, one of the fun parts that made me *me*. The only thing to top my love of fashion and clothing was my love of swimming and being in the water. I could and would spend hours swimming, losing myself in the strokes, cutting through the water and clocking up length after length after length, feeling energised, full of life and totally me.

We all have this inside us. Our thing or things that we love doing, that we enjoy above all others and about which we are confident. The things that make us tick. That give us our own personal buzz and make us who we are. However, after becoming a mum to my first tiny human, the things that I enjoyed, that made me *me*, were obviously put on the back burner – and came to be viewed as indulgent treats rather than normal pastimes. By the time I had our second tiny human eighteen months later, I found myself feeling completely lost and questioning who I was anymore.

Matters came to a head when I found myself on a once-in-forever solo shopping trip, with the only objective being to pick out some nice new clothes for myself. Total bliss, right? No. It was total hell. I wondered around the stores like I was in a foreign universe, not even knowing where to begin when it came to the style of clothes I should be wearing or the styles of clothes that I actually liked. I found myself in the changing room on my own, arms full of clothes and eyes full of tears as I sat wondering what the hell I was supposed to be looking good in or even liking.

Yes, it suddenly dawned on me that since creating life I was no longer able to create awesome-looking outfits, though the feeling ran so much deeper than this. I'd actually lost my enjoyment of something I used to love doing and I'd lost the ability just to enjoy me being me, with no pressure or responsibility for anyone else – for the afternoon, at least. It dawned on me that I no longer knew what made me *me*. That scared the hell out of me and made me feel the most vulnerable and unconfident I had felt in years.

This lack of confidence about who I actually was ran through all areas of my life as a new mum. From socialising but being worried sick that I had nothing other than sleep schedules, sore nipples and poo for conversation, to going back to work, where I felt like the new kid starting at a new school, as faces had changed, people had moved on and up to different roles. I remember not being able even to remember where my desk was – and it took me a good few months until I started to feel anywhere near confident that I was getting back into the workflow and actually knew what the hell I was doing.

It all made me realise that it takes time and patience, coupled with a little bit of soul-searching, to figure out what we now want our life to look like and who we want to be in it. It also takes the acknowledgement and acceptance that we cannot rewind and get back the old life we had before our tiny humans arrived – and most importantly, that this is OK. But how do we mould this new life and what on earth does it look like?

I know for me that this new life as a mum and figuring out how I now fit into the world at large is still a work in progress, five years into motherhood. Over the last year I have started to make a conscious effort to look after myself more and to start awarding importance to my own wants and needs. I've started to regain my sense of style and love of fashion, and have come to realise that my core identity is not too different to how it was pre-motherhood, that I am still me. I've created a new career thanks to my writing and even though I still have moments (sometimes daily) where I doubt my ability and feel that I'm going to be found out and slammed as a terrible writer, I am ploughing on regardless and excited about where all of this may lead. And regardless of whether this book is a massive success or not, I am so grateful for the process it has taken me through because it's played a huge part in leading me back to what makes me *me*.

So, if you are currently questioning how to be you again, there is one important thought to hold onto. Yes, the world has moved on; yes, you have been unsure of your footing in it; and yes, your life can sometimes look so different to where you started off that you don't even recognise how you ended up here. But here you are, turning up to it every day and doing a damn fine job at creating this technicolour, beautiful chaos in which you are now living and loving. The old you is looking at you with awe and pride at what you have achieved so far.

The old you thinks this new you is pretty fantastic!

It's time you started too as well.

WHICH MUM WORKS THE HARDEST?

I have been a stay-at-home mum, a back-to-work mum and a work-from-home mum. I've dreaded going back to work to the point of feeling sick to the stomach and waking in a sweaty panic at the thought of it in the middle of the night. I've longed to go back to work, counting down the days to have a break from the monotony of being a mum. And I have run myself ragged trying to balance the work-from-home mum solution that sees you trying to work and get stuff done whilst ignoring the mountains of housework, dirty washing and toys surrounding me.

It's fair to say that I've tried most work scenarios since becoming a mum-of-two and all of them are as rewarding, as guilt-inducing, as challenging and as exhausting as each other – just for different reasons. Therefore, I have the utmost respect for all mums whatever they conclude is the best decision for them, their family and their situation. Let's face it, the decision of whether or not we go back to work isn't purely down to what we simply fancy doing with the rest of our lives. There are financial, logistical and emotional factors all at play and each has implications that are more far-reaching than the wage packet.

THE BACK-TO-WORK MUM

Ooh, going back to work after growing a tiny human raises a plethora of challenging emotions and guilty thoughts, as you lurch from joy at the thought of drinking HOT coffee with actual real-life adults to screaming at your partner/boss/anyone who will listen: 'I'M NOT GOING BACK: I DON'T CARE IF WE ARE FACING FINANCIAL RUIN: I DON'T CARE IF WE HAVE TO MOVE IN WITH YOUR PARENTS. I'M NOT GOING BACK AND YOU CAN'T MAKE ME.' (Plus, whilst you were out working I've handcuffed myself to the tiny human on the sofa, and the next-door neighbour's dog has swallowed the key.)

I never really thought about the concept of going back to work much whilst pregnant with my first tiny human. I'd always had a job from the age of thirteen, and I had a successful career under my belt. A career that made me incredibly proud, that I loved and enjoyed. So I never considered that I would want to give up my career after having a tiny human and be a stay-at-home mum. However, six months after having her, I was getting ready to go back to work and I was filled with anxiety and dread at the thought of leaving her, and started to throw my very own back-to-work tantrum that went a little something like this:

MY BACK-TO-WORK TANTRUM

'The thought of going back to work makes me want to flee the country with my tiny human, never to return again!'

I DON'T want to go back to work. I DON'T want to put my precious tiny human into childcare. I DON'T want to put a brave face on it and I DON'T want to be cool about it. I HATE IT! I HATE IT! I BLOODY WELL HATE IT! And you know what? I don't care less who knows!

I admit it, my stomach lurches with dread at the thought of returning to work and my heart drops at the thought of dropping my little girl off at nursery – even in spite of the fact that I know that she loves it there and is flourishing because of it. However, these feelings are there nonetheless and there is many a day where you can find us sitting outside the nursery gates, Thelma and Louise-style, with me asking my tiny human, 'Hey, how about we sack off this nursery malarkey and do a runner to the park instead?'.

I'm also not afraid to say that I am dreading the thought of returning to work. Oh yes, work in my mind is now some far off place which I am hoping will miraculously disappear forever – or at least until the idea of going back to it doesn't leave me in cold sweats in the middle of the night!

'God, get a grip!' I can hear some of you shouting. But you know what? That is exactly what I am sick of doing. Throughout our journey with motherhood and through some of the most daunting and nigh-on impossible decisions we are faced with making – giving up breast-feeding, going back to work, putting our babies into childcare – we tell ourselves to get a grip or to put a brave face on it. Well, I for one am sick of this and want to have a good old rant instead and say: Why the hell do we need to get a grip and what's so great about a brave face anyway?

Don't get me wrong, I know that us getting a grip is one of our many well-honed, coping techniques and that these skills ensure we get through whatever motherhood chooses to throw at us. I also know that going back to work can be a necessity for financial reasons and/ or to feel like our old selves again. However, I've come to realise that we also sometimes just need to be able to vent to no one in particular about how goddam horrid we feel about it.

Yes, I had a job I enjoyed before the tiny humans came along. Yes, I like to class myself as a strong and independent woman. Yes, I like earning money. And yes, I can sometimes be found climbing the walls longing for Mr Tumble not to be my only form of adult conversation. Despite all of this, there are moments where all I want to do is shut the doors and windows to my cosy home, snuggle up my tiny humans, put a bun (of the Mary Berry kind) in the oven and decorate a loo roll with tiny painted fingertips.

I guess what myself and my mummy tantrum are trying to say is that, rather than being strong and brave through it all, wouldn't it sometimes be a refreshing relief to admit how hard all parenting decisions are and how we dread having to make them? Wouldn't it be pure mummy bliss to admit our fears in all of their technicolour glory to anyone who will listen, without fear of judgement or ridicule or being told to get a grip? You see, what I'm finding with this journey through motherhood is that it is a world of contradictions and hidden meanings. It is a world to be celebrated and it is a place where sometimes the bravest thing of all is to admit how fearful and un-brave we actually feel. It takes guts to share how we are spending our nights racked with anxiety and sheer panic over a decision we have to make for our children and how during these particular moments we wish we could cocoon ourselves and our tiny humans from the big bad world and the necessity of tough decisions.

Therefore, all you amazing mums picking your way through the minefield that is deciding to go back to work, deciding to stay at home, deciding to put your child into day care for the first time or deciding on any other of the thousands of tough mummy decisions we have to make daily – let's all say to hell with the brave face and opt for putting on an honest face instead!

It turns out that this is the bravest face of all!

In the meantime, if you happen to see a grown woman and a tiny human dressed in leopard print absconding from the local school gates and heading in the direction of the nearest swing set – please look the other way or feel free to join us.

MY TOP FEARS OF RETURNING TO WORK

Despite my fears and anxieties about returning to work for the first time after having my first tiny human, I found that by the time I was due back, when she was ten months old, I was starting to look forward to it. To having a slice of life back that was mine, independent of my role as mum and wife. Add into that the very idea of being able to drink actual hot coffee and think only about myself, and all of a sudden being back at work a few days a week didn't seem so awful. However, like the rest of the mums returning back to work, I still had some major concerns and genuine fears. Therefore, with a dash of 'how the hell am I going to pull this off' humour, I'm hoping that sharing my tongue-in-cheek list of fears below will bring a smile of recognition to every mum currently gearing themselves up to get their head back into the game of work.

1. Will there be coffee? And will it be HOT? Oh, and can I drink it without someone hugging my kneecaps and slamming their head into my fanny?

2. Will I be lonely going to the toilet on my own? Who will babble at me, sit on my lap and cover me in dribble and shredded pieces of sucked and spat-out toilet paper?

3. Will I remember that my name isn't actually Mum? Dammit, how will I know when someone is actually talking to me unless they are using the m-word? In fact, what is my name?

4. How will I cope with the silence? I wonder if they would mind playing a mashup of CBeebies in the background accompanied by the sounds of cats being strangled on repeat, just so I can concentrate?

5. How will I handle being clean ALL day? I wonder if I could get John from Purchasing to pebbledash me with spat-out cheese sarnie on his lunch break? Or would that be too much like bordering on a weird sexual act that's not appropriate for the workplace?

6. If I don't have a gazillion bits of plastic crap to hurdle over, pick up or tread on with bare, unsuspecting feet, how will I ever get in my exercise quota? I'll tell you what, I'll ask Sally from HR to go and empty a multipack of drawing pins and paperclips around my desk with a few open-mouthed staplers for good measure. Yes, that should do it. Oh, and if every time I attempt to approach my desk someone could jump on my back, wrap their arms around my neck in a chokehold whilst shouting 'Giddy up, mummy,' that would be awesome!

7. What the hell will I talk about? It's been so long since I had an actual adult conversation that didn't centre around wiping bums, sleep schedules and how much wine is really too much. Shit, what do people even talk about now? I must make a note to try and stay awake tonight and watch the news for the first time in eighteen months.

8. In fact, what the hell do people even wear these days? Will leggings pebbledashed with porridge and worn out at the knees, and anything resembling clean (ish) thrown over them, pass the work wardrobe test?

9. Oh shit, do I really have to go back?

THE STAY-AT-HOME MUM

I went back to work, but things change, life happens and sometimes, no matter how much you need to return to work to help with family finances or follow your own personal career ambitions, other stuff just gets in the way and makes it impossible. For me and for us as a family, once we'd ventured down the one-way path of two tiny humans just eighteen months apart and two ongoing battles with PND and postpartum psychosis, it became clear that returning to my high-flying cushty career in Geneva was a dead end. I was just not well enough to deal with the emotional strains of keeping my mental shit together, whilst planning the childcare logistics of two under two and keeping a global client happy and convinced I was still up to the job.

Something had to give, and I wasn't prepared for it to be my mind. So I became a stay-at-home mum for the first time. I have to admit to you that pre-motherhood, I thought the role of a stay-at-home-mum was easier than going to work. I had rose-tinted visions of what it meant and what it would look like: spending hazy sunny days hanging out with my tiny human, enjoying endless walks, belly giggles and daytime TV. No sign of a dirty nappy, mountain of washing, sleepless night or a feeling of loneliness and lack of fulfilment. And if I'm honest, after years of loving and thriving on my busy and creative career, I found that I was looking forward to having a break from it and having my role be that of 'mum'.

However, that's the thing with preconceptions, they bite you in the arse – royally!

Overnight, I went from career mum, batting off the guilt-inducing questions of 'What? You've gone back to work already?' and 'How many days do you have her in childcare for?', as well as comments such as 'I'm so lucky, I don't have to work' to now batting off the guilt-inducing questions of 'Oh, so you don't work?' and 'What do you do all day?', alongside comments such as 'Wow, being at home with two under two must drive you crazy!', 'I bet you wish you could go back to work for a break!' and 'I'm so lucky I have my career to keep me sane and keep me from not feeling like "just" a mum'.

No win-win situation, I tell you!

THE WORK FROM HOME MUM

Even when I mixed my role of stay-at-home mum and career mum and became a work-from-home mum, the guilt-laden and insensitive questions and comments remained. Oh, so you're a writer? How on earth can you do that properly with the kids running around? How do you get anything done? I bet you feel like you're not doing anything to your full potential. Are you published yet? Oh you're not. Wow, so you're not earning anything from your writing but you're spending every spare minute doing it rather than folding the washing, cleaning the bath and taking proper care of your kids? God, that must be a HUGE financial burden for your hubby.

Kill me now!

The thing that I've found that increases the hurt conjured by all these questions is the raw fact that they all leave us questioning our self-worth.

It was one day of feeling like a particularly worthless work-from-home mum, trying to juggle looking after two tiny humans under two with following my dreams of being a writer, that I wrote the following section in my journal to vent how frustrated I was feeling. I had just finished a conversation with my husband about our different roles and how they were both as equally important as each other (despite only one earning a wage), which made me realise that the only person questioning my self-worth was me – and that I had to do something about it. I had to start realising that my role is a worthy one. That what I do, despite its lack of financial reward, is of great importance. That I am worthy.

YOU ARE WORTHY!

I am no longer a main breadwinner. I am no longer bringing home the readies, BUT I AM OF VALUE and what I do is of GREAT WORTH. You may now be the primary breadwinner, but I am the primary caregiver. I am the fount of all tiny-pieces-of-plastic-crap knowledge. My boardroom may now be the bomb site that used to be our kitchen, my new clients may now be on the slightly younger *can't speak or wipe their own tiny arses* size, but I deserve the same respect that was awarded me when I won a new account or nailed a client presentation.

I deserve this respect because I earn it 24/7 of every goddam day. I do not begrudge the fact that I have children or the fact that I have a new role, but I do resent anyone who does not see my role as important or doesn't see me as worthy of receiving full respect for it.

However, as well as teaching others this, I need to teach myself to respect what I do, to be fierce about my new role and my achievements in the same ways I once was when wearing my latest office outfit and presenting strategy to my peers.

My new role is one that has involved a complete transformation – of mind, body, emotions and life. It is a role I live and breathe, as it is one that requires me to be at work and on duty twenty-four hours a day, seven days a week. In this role, I am indispensable. The shit WILL hit the fan if I am not around, and there is no one else who can do my job better than me.

My payment is in smiles, kisses, tantrums, daily fails and daily wins that before now would have seemed insignificant but which now mean more than significance itself. It is a role that leaves me feeling exhausted and spent. It makes me at times feel like I am failing spectacularly and at other times like I could run the universe. It is the most important role I have ever had but it leaves me feeling that this role of such magnitude is not rewarded with the importance it deserves. The importance I deserve. Instead, it is implied that the role in itself is not enough but needs to be supplemented by other more worthy roles, jobs or successes, since this most important role is no more than a hobby. For if I am 'just' doing this role, then I am not working hard enough, I am not fulfilling my true potential and I am letting my real hopes and dreams fall by the wayside because of it.

I would like to say on behalf of every mum out there that motherhood is not a hobby. It is not a sideline project to run alongside the main event. It is not a fun activity you can pick up and fit into your otherwise more important and worthwhile enterprises. Motherhood is the main event and as mums – stay-at-home mums, career mums or work-from-home mums – we somehow have to work out how to shoehorn our hopes, dreams, desires and careers in around it. There is no off switch, weekends off or downtime. For those of us who run our careers and businesses alongside motherhood, there is no let-up on the mothering role. It remains the same, the workload trebles and we deal with it and move on, in the best state we can. Unlike other new jobs we find we do not replace one with the other. Instead we (somehow) juggle the two, let go of some of the expectations, increase others and reluctantly learn to compromise – and then suck up the guilt that this compromise evokes. No matter what we do as mums – go back to work, stay at home or work from home – it's difficult, challenging, rewarding, exhausting and exhilarating in its own right. However, we should never lose sight of the fact that working or not does not make us more or less worthy mums. Just because we don't work outside the home does not mean what we do is worth less.

We are women, we are mums, we are pioneers, we are caregivers, we are trying our damn best, we are fighting social and personal battles to triumph for ourselves and our families.

WE, my friends, are WORTHY!

CHAPTER 15

POST-BABY BODY

BODY CONFIDENCE VERSUS BODY BULLSHIT

Right, let me be the first to tell you this little nugget of truth. You don't have to fit into your pre-baby jeans, days, weeks, months, years even after exiting a tiny human out of your body. Hell, you don't have to fit back into those spray-on tight, muffin-top splurging, camel toe creating garments ever again – and you know what? This does not make you a lazy, unfit, unhealthy crap mother and a disgrace to all womankind! I know, who knew, right?

And, yes I know I'm going against the perfectly preened, honed and toned grain of the media and crazy social media world at large with their perfect images of the perfect pre- and post-baby bodies. However, another secret I'm going to dare to tell the truth about is that none of the stuff we see in the magazines and online is real anyway. It's all a pile of airbrushed and perfectly filtered baloney to make pages of magazines, Instagram accounts and Facebook feeds look pretty. It's Narnia, it's Disney, its Santa fucking Claus, it's not real.

And you know what? As long as we keep sight of this, then we are all going to be OK . . . Aren't we?

God, it's hard, isn't it, to remain strong and resolute in this way of thinking, because we have been surrounded by and indoctrinated with these pictures since the beginning of our time. Pictures of a fake reality, in which everything and everyone in it is airbrushed within an inch of their lives. I mean, for God's sake, even the dolls we played with as little girls, had a waist size that was anatomically incorrect and genetically impossible without removing three ribs. All topped off with the perfect skin, hair, a pair of perky boobs and a set of Hollywood white teeth that Simon Cowell and Rylan would fight tooth and perfectly manicured nail for.

So, you know what, my lovely friend? I don't blame us for looking in the mirror on one of our wobbly thigh days and, instead of feeling empowered, feeling a bit inadequate and like we don't meet the standards that we have been expected to meet for the majority of our lives. But, please listen up, lovely, these standards are bullshit, their foundations based on an airbrushed, non-existent reality. These images have been lying to us for decades and even now as grown women, looking at these images and knowing they are not reality, that the person in the picture does not really look like this, that we should brush it off and treat it for what it is – a picture that needs to look pretty rather than real to make us buy whatever they are peddling – there is still a part in our well-educated minds and the self-conscious teenage corner of our hearts that has us wondering, no matter how briefly, 'Why don't I look like that?'.

It plants the poisonous and unfounded seed in even the most confident of us that we need to exercise more, we need to make more time to look more polished, we need to be, well, more.

This negative way of viewing our bodies and our appearances is compounded by the sad reality that after our bodies fulfil their beautiful potential and produce another human being, we are at our lowest and most insecure rather than feeling the most empowered and the most beautiful. And isn't this just all sorts of wrong?

I'm not saying I was or am immune to this hell. I've brought into this perfect body charade since as long as I can remember. I brought the magazines, flicked through the glossy pages adorned with glossy hair and skin, feeling nothing but awe and a burning desire to one day look like that, to have a figure like that, skin like that. And when I finally did look like that, I would finally be . . . be what? Feel what? Happy? Accomplished? Like I'd finally made it? And had proved myself?

Hand on heart, I have looked at these magazines over the years and made myself all of the following soulless promises.

By the time I was twenty-five I would be a comfortable size 8 (not just a fluke size 8 because I've had a bug for the last week). By the time I was thirty I would have a six pack and arms like Jennifer Anniston.

And these promises seeped out and carried themselves forward into my pregnancy and motherhood. I will have toned legs and arms throughout my pregnancy, I will not get stretch marks, I will get into shape as soon as I can post-baby, I will not let myself go, I will be back into my jeans before you know it, I will look like those mums I've seen in the magazines, on social media feeds and on bright, shiny parenting blogs. These mums are obviously doing a fantastic job, they are owning motherhood. These mums are what mums should look like . . . these mums are happy and together.

I brought into the fake reality and pressure following the birth of my first tiny human, desperate to prove to myself and the world at large that motherhood hadn't changed me. I needed to look like those mums I'd seen and read about so much. Because, God forbid, if I didn't, the whole world would think I was not coping, I was not cut out for the game of motherhood.

I really put an emphasis on 'bouncing back'. I realise now it wasn't so much about the actual pounds lost, but rather was intermingled and tangled up with the desire to bounce back, to snap back into the old me, my old life, to bounce back and bounce back as quickly as possible. It was almost like it was a race, a test to see how quickly after growing a tiny human I could get back to normal, fit back into my old life, get back my old body and fit back into those godforsaken pre-baby jeans – a symbol that I'd arrived.

We all feel a bit like this, don't we? Even despite towing the rational line of thought in front of others, and insisting that 'of course we realise it's going to take time to shift the baby weight, we're not going to do anything too soon', there is that little voice in our head goading us to go and try on our pre-baby jeans just so we can gauge just how long our bounce back is going to take.

Well, I am here to tell you that we all need to stop this shit right now. We need to back away from the scales, the skinny jeans and the ridiculous images of what we are told a 'perfect' mum looks like, because you know what? You, me, and every other mum out there are already enough. We are already perfection personified with our stretch marks, thread veins, slighter softer edges. We are beautiful. Take a look at your beautiful self. A long good look and remind yourself that you are already enough.

MY PRE-BABY JEANS CAN GO F*** THEMSELVES

(To be read when you can't even fit your big toe let alone your leg into these goddam mofos – aka your pre-baby, *I ain't ever getting my arse into them bastards again so pass me a biscuit* jeans.)

Look at you, hanging there, looking all fabulous, not a seam out of place. All neat and sexy, acting like the queen jeffing bee. All elongated lines and unstretched to perfection waistline, taunting me and making me feel like I never even knew you, let alone was once able to wear you out in public.

What is it about our pre-baby jeans that drive us so goddam, batshit crazy post-baby? Six weeks – yes, ladies, SIX ridiculous weeks after pushing a tiny human out of my vagina – I was trying to push my swollen elephant calves and bits into my pre-baby jeans. There they were, taunting me from the back of the wardrobe, making me stupidly think that if I squinted at them with one eye closed, whilst standing at a feng shui angle at the other side of the bedroom, they would actually still fit me, no problemo. The evil seed was planted and before you know it, there I was, ripping off my maternity leggings and trying to coax my postpartum body into my pre-baby skinny jeans. What the hell was I thinking and what the hell was I trying to prove?

God knows.

But I'll tell you what I did prove to myself by this ridiculous act:

a) that NO mum should attempt to go anywhere near pre-baby jeans until at least twelve months postpartum

and

b) that denim really does catch fire quite quickly.

POST-BABY BODY INSTASHAMING

OK, so I am just going to put it out there and say it, NO HOLDS BARRED . . .

I CANNOT STAND BEFORE BUMP versus POSTPARTUM PHOTOS

#fookoff #whocares #bullshit

S.E.R.I.O.U.S.L.Y.

Social media is flooded with these visual statements from fellow mums posting pics of themselves postpartum, making a point of always standing sideways, always in pristine gym gear of the obligatory skimpy but classy sporty underwear that says fit and healthy mum – and definitely not body-shaming exhibitionist.

They are always detailed with how many weeks postpartum (the fewer the weeks, the louder we tweet 'WOW LOOK AT HER ABS') and always make other mums want to comment #fuckyoubiach.

Why do we need to see these pics? And, more importantly, why do we feel the need to share them with the rest of the world at large?

Now before you call the McJudgey pants police on me or try the feminist edged reply of: 'I'm empowering other women. I'm showing them that they too can look like this postpartum', I would just like to stop you there and say: BALONEY!

I don't believe you.

I've heard all the statements, along the lines of 'I'm celebrating the amazing thing that my body has done by sharing it, dressed in my undercrackers with a million other people in the hope that I get . . .'

Get what, is what I would like to ask? What is it that we as a society hope to get from it?

That is the real crux of the question.

As a mum of two tiny humans with quite a good post-baby body – i.e. one that still works, only leaks wee involuntarily if I sneeze really hard or miscalculate the height of my star jump on the bouncy castle at the local soft play, one that is strong enough to carry a tantruming two-and-a-half-year-old and a sulky four-year-old AT THE SAME TIME – I never once felt the need to post pics of my tummy nine weeks after pushing a tiny human out of my vagina.

I am a feminist and a huge fan and champion of fellow females. Therefore, I am all for empowering women and celebrating the quite frankly awesome roles our bodies do and feel there is nothing more beautiful than a woman who is comfortable and confident in her own skin and encouraging other women to celebrate their own bodies in all their glorious, technicolour shapes and sizes.

But, I don't buy that this style of posts and images are an example of that. I don't buy that the main aim of them is to lift up other women and celebrate all bodies regardless of shape, muscle definition or length of postpartum progress. I don't believe that their purpose is a true and honest celebration of the female form or a confidence boost to other mums, a much-needed form of 'mummy motivation'.

They just make me question, 'Why?'.

Why does someone feel the need to share these quite intimate pictures of themselves? I'm not saying you should never take pics of yourself pre- and postpartum to document how mad and crazy it is that your skin can stretch to the size of a continent and then back again like a humungous skin tsunami wave. Take them, save them to show your tiny humans the magnificence of the female body so when they are older they can see what an extraordinary, amazing and strong body their mummy has.

But what is the point of showing them to others, complete strangers in particular, on the Internet?

And why title the pics 'Look at me, bouncing back three weeks postpartum' #fitmum #noexcuses #gettothegym #notlazy.

Aggghhhhh! I just want to hashtag the hell out of these posts with a big fat #whocares.

Now, don't get me wrong, I'm all for mums looking after our health and keeping our mind and bodies strong. I love the feeling and freedom of being able to run without tiny humans hanging off my ankles and taking a slice of me-time through exercise. It does my body good, but most importantly it keeps my mind strong.

What I don't buy into is the reasoning behind why a fellow mum would feel the need to post such pics under titles such as 'Bouncing back after just three weeks' or 'Wow, I'm already back into my skinny jeans' and then plaster them all over social media for strangers and fellow mums who may also happen to be three weeks postpartum to see and compare themselves to.

Now, this is where I have to make a little confession here and be completely, toe-curlingly honest with you. I once wrote a Facebook status that read:

'3 months in and back in my skinny jeans'

(#whataknob)

And I'm now going to be even more nails-down-a-blackboard honest with you. (This is killing me to admit this to you, since I fear you will want to break either our friendship or my neck, but it is so important to share this with you.)

That post did not come from a good place. I did not do it to empower other mums. To help other mums celebrate their bodies. To motivate. No, I was doing it to show off, to say to the world, 'Look at me, I had a baby only twelve weeks ago and I've already snapped back into my Size 10 jeans – look at me go!'. This was obviously proof of what a great yummy mummy, hot wife, sexy friend, all-round amazing human being I am. In fact, scrap that, what an amazing SUPERhuman being I am.

Here I am. Having it all – the baby, the hubby, and the skinny bloody jeans to boot. Motherhood has not set me back. Oh no, I am still keeping all my shit together, I am acing all the new mum malarkey, taking it all in my stride. Breezing through the sleepless nights, loving every minute of it and look, I am back in my skinny jeans to prove what a skinny legend I am.

What a knob, ladies and gents, what a bloody knob!

So, you see, there you have it. I know first hand what these type of posts mean because I've been their author. However, I am honest enough not to bullshit you about me doing it to motivate and celebrate other mums and their postpartum bodies. I am ripping off the skinny jeans plaster and admitting the dark, narcissistic and, quite frankly, unhealthy place this post came from. And come on, if we are all honest we can all admit to some degree that this ugly little corner exists in all of our minds and personalities. If not, then I simply don't believe you. We all want to show the world (particularly after becoming a mum) that we are doing a good job, that no, motherhood has not fazed us. That we are carrying on as normal just with a baby slotted into our lives. That we are all over this new life like a knackered mum over a lie-in.

Posting up pics of how we've bounced back, giving ourselves #noexcuses and then hiding it under the raison d'être of wanting to motivate other mums is doing a disservice to every mum – hell, every woman – out there.

You see, what we don't acknowledge is that it just makes the majority of other mums feel a bit crap. It makes other mums question why they are not #bouncingback. It gets them questioning what their #excuses are for not going on a run and bench-pressing their babies until toned to perfection. It generally smacks of the competitive edge, still too sharp to touch, from our playground days.

I don't know why we do it to ourselves and each other. Why we feed this ridiculous pressure, and add to the images portrayed in the media, by believing in the perfect wife and perfect mother with her perfect wardrobe that hangs perfectly off a perfect body. Again, all total BALONEY, my friend.

And what's more, posting pics up and statements hidden under the claim of offering motivation is just fuelling the perfect body propaganda that we have all been enduring for the majority of our existence – and trying to ignore for fear of becoming unhealthily obsessed with every inch of our bodies, sucking on a piece of lettuce and believing that if we could just get back into our skinny jeans then everything will be right in the world.

NO. NO. A million times, NO.

Let's stop the instashaming and just instead ask ourselves before we make a post celebrating our weight loss, our postpartum bellies, our squeezing back into our pre-baby skinny jeans: What place is this coming from? Let's answer it and then ask ourselves the question again – but this time let's all answer it honestly, no matter how much the answer touches a raw nerve in the grimier, less exposed part of our minds. No matter how much the answer makes us squirm. No matter if the answer makes us feel a bit of a dick.

Then, if our honest-to-god, hand-on-heart answer is anything other than 'To provide a positive body image message to empower myself and other women out there', let's do all of ourselves a favour and just not post it. Instead save the pics, show them to our partners, print them off, stick them to our fridges and use them for our own personal motivation – not to deplete that of others.

As fellow mums and women, we have a responsibility to lift each other up. To support each other, to encourage and say, 'You know what, it's OK'. No judgement! Let's make it our personal mission to weave this mission into our everyday lives, from conversations in the park, comments at the school gates and the dialogue we put out there on social media.

Let's make it so we are responsible for celebrating each other's successes rather than failures and showing how beautiful we are when we stand together in support. And let's all remember that the most important part of our body that we need to be fit is our minds.

CHAPTER 16

THE EVERY MUM GUIDE TO BEING A DAD

DADS, YOU'RE NOT JUST SPERM DONORS!

Yes, I know it's a bit bloody rich for me to sit here and claim that I can talk about fatherhood, especially as I have a vagina. However, bear with me and my knackered self for just a moment. You see, one of my missions with this book is to bridge the gaps between all the areas of parenthood, to speak about all the issues we face – no judgement and no fear. So I would just like to put this idea out there: if as partners we spoke openly to each other about all the stuff that was getting under our skin, about all the crap that we feel we can't talk about to each other but which is widening the gap of irritation between us then, then wow, our lives as exhausted and bewildered parents would be a damn sight easier. And if not easier, then at least more fun and with more chances of sexual encounters!

I believe passionately that dads (like us mums) need a support network, need a voice and, most importantly, need to be heard. Bringing a tiny human into the world has a profound effect on the men in our lives too. Dads are not just babysitters. Shock horror, they can be trusted to care for their own flesh and blood. They have certain areas of this parenting malarkey down better than us mums. And given everything motherhood throws at us, we would be lost without them.

Yes, some dads are a bit shit and some are total arseholes, but so are some mums. Being parents is the most challenging thing we will all ever do together and yes, some of us don't make it out the other side still together. But let's at least give ourselves a fighting chance by being honest about how we are feeling, no matter how ugly. Lets' own this parenting malarkey and not let the fooker take us down!

IT'S A S*** FIGHT FOR NEW DADS TOO

When it comes to parenthood us mums get the raw end of the deal, going through labour and then all the recovery, emotions and hormones we have to deal with afterwards. However, those poor bastards otherwise known as the daddies have to put up with a hell of a lot too, just without any of the recognition.

Pregnancy and parenthood is like a grand theatre production where us women and our bumps take centre stage from the moment the curtain goes up. Yes, your partner may be awarded the role of supporting actor during the pregnancy, but once your bundle of joy bursts onto the scene he will be lucky if he is allowed the title of janitor. While everyone and their nan is cooing over you and the baby, telling you how great you look and how well you have done, your poor bloke will be looking on from the sidelines screaming, 'I wasn't just a sperm donor!'.

No 'Well done! You donated good genes', no 'How are you feeling?' and no offers of advice on how to fathom out the bewildering world of fatherhood. Instead, they are left to figure it out for themselves, hope for the best and then get themselves back to work.

As we mums, albeit sitting on a rubber ring or ice pack, are trying to figure out our new role in life and get our heads around the responsibility of motherhood, so too is he. You see, parenthood has also happened to him. He, like ourselves, has also been flung into a whole new world of the unknown. He too has a new role in life that he needs to get his head and heart around. Yes, he may not have pushed a baby out of a vagina, but he saw his best friend and the one person he loves most in the world push one out of theirs – pretty bloody terrifying!

We have months to try and get our head around childbirth and the new position of mummy. Months to talk to our growing tiny human and share plans, creating an infinite bond that will never break. For we already know and love our tiny human before they get here. We have read all the numerous books on motherhood in preparation and signed up to all the mum and baby forums. We therefore have a huge head start. By contrast, when the baby arrives, he has just a couple of weeks with you full time to try and catch up to where you are before he then has to leave his new family bubble and head back out to work and into normality.

For him, nothing has changed on the face of things. His body is still the same and his bits have not been stretched to oblivion. He may not bear the marks of bringing a tiny human into the world, but he also has his own set of challenges to overcome – and all without a parenting book or support group in sight.

We all know the pressures we face as mums, but does anyone ever stop long enough to consider the pressures faced by the new dads in our lives? And, more importantly, to ask them if they also need a vent, a glass of wine or a bit of support?

We are not the only ones with anxieties about being a parent and challenges to our own identity. We are just the ones more able to talk about it and with more avenues to do so. We are not the only ones who are figuring out our relationship with our tiny human and how best to look after them. However, by the very nature of carrying them for nine months and by being their mum, we are the ones who have the last word on their care, from what they are wearing through to when and how they are fed. We as mums are in the driving seat and we have the majority of the control, which can at times leave the dads twiddling their thumbs and feeling a bit redundant.

We may feel as though we have lost ourselves along the way and are struggling to remember our pre-baby self, but he is there also feeling lost and struggling to find the right words to help you navigate your way through the new mum fog. We think he doesn't understand – and he doesn't understand. How can we expect him to? Though we are on the same journey into parenthood, his path has been a totally different one.

Like our good friend motherhood, fatherhood is a total shit fight. Men worldwide have to juggle getting their head around being a dad, dealing with the financial pressures of providing for his new family and navigating around the hormonal time bombs hidden on every corner. All whilst trying to be a hands-on dad as well as a loving and supportive husband who says all the right things at the right time because, after all, it is his wife who has done all the hard work! It's exhausting and overwhelming – sound familiar?

So let's spare a thought and raise a glass of the strong stuff to all the knackered dads out there, up to their necks in long arse commutes, daddy duties and supporting their wives. You are doing one hell of a job, boys!

WHY US MUMS NEED TO BE MORE DAD

Dads for the majority of time get a bad rap. In fact, the poor bastards for most of their days are fighting a losing battle when it comes to knowing best about parenting. Us mums (rightly and wrongly, depending on what kind of day/sleepless night we have had) rule the roost when it comes to anything tiny human related.

However, I am here to reveal that us mums are missing a bloody trick of the dad variety, and that the key to our mum-shaped lives being less stressful, less guilt-ridden and less knackering is in fact by being more Dad!

Yes, ladies, it's time we channeled our alpha male, plugged into our testosterone channel and pulled on a pair of big dad pants (sexy!)

Here's how to inject more dad into your life:

• Leave the house

YES, just leave the house, no bag in tow, no unnecessary baby paraphernalia. No worries. No problem and no chance your morning outing has now turned into your afternoon one as you are so bogged down with baby crap that you can't get out the bloody door! SERIOUSLY, watching my beloved leave the house with my tinier beloved on an outing was a total bloody epiphany. Here is how his check list went:

Tiny human – check!
Nappy – check!
Wipes – check!
Pre-made bottle – check!
Beer money – check!
Jacket with pockets to put it all in – check!

Out the door in five seconds flat. OK, so that's a lie, more like fifteen minutes after asking me where the nappies were, but STILL he knocked the shit out of my attempts at leaving the house with my baby bag that includes everything we would need if, heaven forbid, a natural disaster hit, aliens landed or zombies attacked, leaving us homeless and with all Tescos looted of nappies and wipes as far as the eye can see. Yes, ladies, we need to up our game when it comes to leaving the house with less crap and replace it with the most important thing (apart from baby) on the dad check list – beer money. Good God, why have I not thought of this before?

• Don't sweat the small stuff

By the small stuff I mean your small tiny human. Apparently in this hip new world of getting your Dad on, no one is going to call Esther Rantzen if you don't give your tiny human a bubble bath every night or even if you commit the sin of all sins and leave it a few nights. I've also experienced the revelation that it's OK if you don't have the monitor turned up to a volume level that lets you (and all hard-of-hearing folk within a three-mile radius of your house) monitor every slight movement your baby makes throughout the night. In fact, in this brave new world, where testosterone not boobs rule the roost, you don't even need a bloody monitor because you can just leave the door of their nursery ajar instead – who knew? The list of crap we worry ourselves with as mums goes on forever, but in the world of Dad, not so much. Yes, I know – total bloody bliss!

• Get yourself some guilt-free me-time

BULLSHIT, I hear you shout and yes, I hear ya, sister! But why the hell not? Why the hell should we not be able to get our knackered little mitts on some of this guilt-free good stuff and enjoy ourselves like the pioneering men in our lives? There is no reason. Yes, I know the biach that is mummy guilt is whispering her propaganda in your ear, attesting the opposite and making you believe that any time spent on things other than dirty bums, puréeing mush, *Wheels on the Bus* reruns and scraping human shit out of your nails means that you are a selfish bitch whore of a mother. Well to hell with it and to hell with you, Mother Nature! You know what? Some days the only thing I want to be scraping out of my unmanicured nails is the chocolate remains from an afternoon tea, or the leftover salt from a tequila slammer. In fact, anything other than another person's poo (even if I grew that aforementioned person). Ladies, grad hold of this awesome pearl of Daddy wisdom and realise that you too deserve some quality time. You too are a person independent of the needs of your little one. Like the Dad in your life, remember that your little one is not going to be scarred for life because you took an hour out to go for a swim/sleep/walk/whatever the hell you want.

• The Delayed Response manoeuvre

Good God, who knew that the speed of light had nothing on the speed a new mum can travel across a Mega Blocks-littered nursery to stem the bleed of a scream? Oh yes, we are all over the shit that is responding to the needs of our little ones with the efficiency that can only be likened to the speed with which we can now crack open, pour and gulp a glass of vino at the end of the day (or mid-morning, depending on the shit that has already gone down). However, have you ever asked yourself why? OK, I know the immediate response is, 'Well, of course, I get to my crying baby as quickly as possible' – but why the panic? The men in our lives seem to operate on more of a wait and delay response. Whilst we are speeding across our bedrooms with our feet barely disturbing the thread of the carpet, panic rising from our gut to the back of our throats, our other halves are yet to emerge from the covers, let alone put on their PJ bottoms, pick up a bottle and saunter to answer the needs of the tiny human. And you know what I realised as I watched this delayed response that my hubby has mastered? No one died. Our little one got their milk and cuddles (albeit a few moments later than usual) and guess what? They went back to sleep, and my hubby sauntered back in and did the same. All whilst I lay wide awake, swimming in a mix of panic and awe at how the men in our life function so differently to us mums. Most importantly, I realised that we need to take a leaf out their book, give ourselves a break and realise that just because we don't perform at lightning speed and answer every beck and call in a nanosecond, we are not failing and the world is not going to come to an end!

• Take a shower without asking

Yes, I know, I know, taking a shower without having to ask permission or make an official announcement is the unicorn of life as a mum. You want to believe in the possibility of it existing but are yet to see evidence! I am here to tell you, it does exist and is being ridden daily by your other half! Come on, girls, utter the magical and affirmative words of 'Honey, I'm off for a shower' and ride that unicorn of bliss that is taking a shower without asking. Grab your towel and indulge in a nice, hot shower. What about the kids? Don't worry, just like they do with you, they will soon let their needs be known to your other half.

• Give less of a shit!

That snide woman at playgroup made some shitty remark about you still breast-feeding? That mum at the school gates gave you and your child a funny look during a tantrum? The mum otherwise known as the Rhyme Time Biach Face made another cutting remark? Ladies, this is where we need to get all Daddy. You see, the men in our lives not only don't give a shit about this type of shit, they don't even notice it exists! It goes completely under their radar – and even if it happens to penetrate their consciousness, they do not award it with anything but a moment's acknowledgement (whether that be disdain, anger or ambivalence) before they move on. Unlike us, who can recall the exact date, time and GPS location on the playground where the incident took place. LET IT GO! MOVE ON! Let's all be more Dad!

• You don't have to look 'hot' to have sex

Contrary to popular belief – or should I say the crap that's shoved down our throats from as early as we can say *Just Seventeen* or *More* magazine – we don't have to look like Giselle to get our leg over our other half. As amazing and sexy as it would be to have every miscellaneous hair on your post-baby body trimmed and in place, tanned legs and manicured digits all ready and prepared for a night of hot sex, let's face it, you could be (and probably are) waiting a hell of a bloody long time before any of that shit gets done and you and your nether regions get any action. Therefore, let's be more Dad about it and just get down to it. Regardless of what you feel you look like, how out of shape you feel or how long it's been since any personal admin took place, remember you have already pulled. He is living with you and will be wanting to have sex with you regardless of all the crap you tell yourself. He loves you and thinks you're hot!

So what are we waiting for you? Let's go find our biggest, sexiest Daddy pants, pull 'em up and Be More Dad! Go on I double Dad dare you!

A LITTLE BIT OF THANKS GOES A LONG WAY

I wrote the following article for my husband after we had our second baby and quite literally had not spoken to each other for what felt like a year thanks to us having our heads up our arses trying to tame the chaos of having two tiny humans under two. It really struck a chord with lots of mums and dads who read my blog, so I wanted to share it with you and all your awesome partners.

What the hell happened to us?

Where have those funny, lovers of life, spur-of-the-moment people gone? You know the ones, they used to laugh together, loved hanging out together and revelled in being the best at looking after each other . . .

Two years and two tiny humans later and I honestly think my hubby could come in with his leg in his hand and I'd ask him if he had managed to put a wash on or hang his coat up! Which has left me asking: 'Am I a heartless biatch?'.

This all came to light, a few months after we had our second little girl, when my hubby put his neck out and was in agony and struggling to move his head, let alone pack up the car, pick up the babies or change a dirty nappy – cue heartless biach alert. I suddenly realised whilst he was reliving the moment of pain to me, still dripping wet (over the bloody kitchen floor which I now had to mop up – gee thanks!), that I was thinking, 'Great, here's to a night of moaning and me having to do bath time on my own!'.

It was my level of irritation that stopped me in my tracks and made me think how different my reaction would have been pre-baby. Firstly, I would have given a shit! Not to say that I don't now, but I would be lying if I claimed to be totally occupied with how he is feeling and what I can do to help. Secondly, I would have run around getting him everything he needed to make him more comfortable, offering a neck rub, pills and sympathy, rather than just feeling annoyed that we were a man down and secretly thinking, 'Is it really that bad?'. Again, cue heartless biach alert!

If I throw total caution to the wind and am completely honest, I just don't have the time for it. I don't have any more energy left to give or any more caring bones in my body that have not already been hijacked and claimed by our two tiny humans.

Cue the question: 'When the hell did this happen to us?' When the hell did we stop giving a damn about each other like how we used to? I hate to admit it, but it was when the second baby came along, delivering us two tiny humans under two. Grateful as we are for them, they have filled every corner of our lives and minds, squashing my hubby and I to the other sides of our new universe, with no time or energy to spare for each other.

It's a difficult one to admit to ourselves, let alone anyone else, that you have slipped into that dreaded cliché of 2.5 children, nagging at each other, worrying about money and falling into bed for nothing more exciting than sleep. It's even harder when you are faced with the unrealistic image of what a happy, harmonious family should be. You know the one, where the successful husband is always home to bath the kids and pour his wife a glass of Chablis, and where the hot mum is equally good at baking toddler-friendly cookies as giving head and scintillating conversation (not at the same time – no one is that good!). They are a couple who, despite having three kids, still find time for date nights and dirty weekends away and just can't wait to have more children because they are just so shit hot at this parenting lark and, in particular, at looking shit hot whilst doing it. We've read the blogs with the glossy and perfect family images whilst we are sat in our puke-stained tracksuit bottoms, pushing a dry shampooed bit of hair out of our knackered faces to get a better look as we ask ourselves: 'Are these parents for real? Is this really what our life should look like?!'.

NO, IT'S NOT!

Who has time to bake cookies let alone factor blow jobs into the equation, and as for scintillating conversation, that's more exhausting than the thought of fellatio. So how the hell do we find the balance between the perfect lives we are fed through the glossy mags and blogs and the reality of what our everyday lives actually look like? And how do we get back to properly caring about our other halves?

Now, without wanting to sound like I am as bad as the rest and trying to bullshit you, I think I may have found the answer and it's so annoyingly simple – believe me, I am so annoyed at myself for not realising it sooner. Getting ourselves back on track starts with two words:

'Thank you.'

Bear with me. If, like me, you think back through any moments when you have wanted to kick the arse of your partner or moments when you have just about had enough, don't they all stem from feeling underappreciated and like all your hard work keeping the babies alive, running the house and juggling the ups and downs of motherhood goes unnoticed and without any thanks? OK, so having your partner say thank you to you for looking after your tiny human all day may seem ridiculous on paper or unnecessary – but just think how great it would make you feel to hear it. And vice versa, saying a thank you to your partner for going out to work, putting out the bins or making dinner may not be ground-breaking or rock and roll, but in its simplest of forms it is showing our best mate, 'our person', that they are appreciated and that we notice them.

I admit it I feel like I am run ragged most days and that my life is now all about other people. Don't get me wrong, I chose to have children and love the bones of them, but sometimes I just need to hear 'thank you' – and so does my hubby. We and the men in our lives need to know that amongst the madness of this new world we have found ourselves in, and between the wall-to-wall baby paraphernalia and endless sleepless nights, we matter to each other. Out of everyone in the universe we have their back and are thankful to share it all with them, regardless of their stiff necks and your puke-covered track bottoms. If a thank you leads to feeling appreciated, which in turn leads us and our other halves to feeling like we actually care, then before you know it we will be baking cookies and – OK, that's a step too far, but you get where I'm going!

I tell you what, I'll go first. Here goes . . .

Mr Jamie Siegl, MERCI BUCKETS

You ROCK my world xxx

TELL MARVIN GAYE TO JOG ON

OK, so come on, admit it. We've all been there when the only thing we want turned on is the telly and the most exciting thing we are lusting after in the bedroom is four hours of uninterrupted sleep. Therefore, this little rhyme is for all us wannabe lovers if only we weren't too damn tired to be too damn sexy.

(To be read to the tune of the awesome song 'Let's Marvin Gaye and Get it On' by Charlie Puth with Meghan Trainor.)

Tell Marvin Gaye to please jog on
My libido's upped and gone
My pubes are dancing around my knees
I piss my pants every time I sneeze
The only thing I want turned on
Is my TV box set marathon

Tell Marvin Gaye to please jog on
I know we ain't had sex for far too long
But I've been awake for twelve hours straight
My poor tits look like dinner plates
I just need sleep, is that so wrong?

Tell Marvin Gaye to please jog on
There's nowt you can do to turn me on
I'm just knackered and want my bed
Don't make me punch you in the head
Tell Marvin Gaye he's got it wrong

Tell Marvin Gaye to please jog on
My sex drive has long, long gone
I don't mean to be a bore
But I don't want to be ravished against the door
Tell Marvin Gaye he's got it wrong

Tell Marvin Gaye to please jog on
I'm too tired to give you one
You've a spare hand of your own
Just please don't wake me when you groan
Marvin Gaye, now PLEASE jog on

CHAPTER 17

WHAT DOES MOTHERHOOD MEAN TO ME?

So, after all this has been said, done and read, what does motherhood actually mean to me?

This is such a hard question to answer (honestly) and I didn't realise how hard it was until seeing it written out before me.

You see, I can churn out the bog standard and socially acceptable response of 'It's the hardest but most wonderful job in the world. One that I am privileged to be lucky enough to have the honour to carry out.' Or I can offer the jokey 'It means having another human's poo under your fingernails on a daily basis, but I wouldn't change it for the world – and it's now one of the reasons I no longer bite my nails. Hey, every turd-lined cloud, eh?!'.

But neither seem to quite cut it or tell the total truth.

So what does motherhood REALLY mean to me?

To me, motherhood has meant a plethora of things, ranging from the hilariously disgusting and heart-stoppingly beautiful to the mind-shatteringly exhausting and at times downright petrifying.

It has made me feel that life and its capabilities are the most profound and magical we could ever dare dream possible. It's filled my heart with a joy I never knew existed, let alone knew that I was capable of feeling, and has given me a new meaning to my life, one that words are too mortal to explain.

It has enriched my life. It has changed me forever. It has given me a new skill set and two tiny purposes who I would now be lost without. They are now as vital to my survival as any other one of my major life-giving organs.

It has made me stronger, braver, more courageous, more ambitious than I have ever been. It has given my life meaning but has also taught me how easily I would give it up if it meant they kept theirs.

As well as building and strengthening my personal kingdom, motherhood has also been the cause of its downfall.

Motherhood has at times meant my darkest of days. It has meant me questioning the very essence of who I am. It has rendered me lost. It has at times meant me being more insecure, more isolated, more uncertain than I have ever been before in my life.

Motherhood has meant me feeing I'm not good enough. Not up to the job. Not worthy of the title Mum. And it would be fair to say that motherhood has made me and broken me in equal measure.

With this knowledge and with my own personal experiences in mind, if I am going to explain honestly what motherhood REALLY means to me right here, right now, this is what I would say:

Motherhood to me means gloriously chubby fingers reaching desperately for mine. Salty dribble-filled kisses and being the only thing they need. Belly laughs and grubby faces. Ice cream smiles, dirty knees and tiny socks. Exhaustion, excitement and endless questions. Nightlong cuddles and sleep-starved nights. Creating our own destiny, dens and visits to the doctor. Bath times, park walks, tantrums galore and bedtime stories. It's where I am at my most challenged whilst experiencing the brightest of times. It has pushed me to my limits and shown me a love that has none.

In it's simplest of terms . . .

Motherhood to me means . . .

EVERYTHING.

EVERY MUM DESERVES THE RIGHT
TO ENJOY MOTHERHOOD

'The world is our stage' has never rung so true since becoming a mum. Even behind the sanctuary of closed doors at home, I still hear myself talking as if 'they' are watching and scoring me on my motherly skills and prowess. (I have no clue who they are.)

Five years into my role as mummy, I still get to the end of the day and score myself on the performance I've managed to pull off that day at being a mum. Did I do all the things on my list which make me feel like I'm a good mum, that I am doing a good enough job? My list covers a multitude of mummy goals which I feel I need to achieve to ensure that my tiny humans have had a well-balanced day and grow into well-balanced, happy and healthy people.

I continue to do this . . . daily . . . and the worst part, apart from the obvious fact of spending my whole day in a blind panic trying to achieve them all, is that I find myself judging myself and deciding whether or not I've been a good mum that day, that week, that year!

I only have to read comments on my blog and Facebook groups to know that there are thousands of us mums putting ourselves under this pressure every single day. Quite literally thousands of mums, whose enjoyment of motherhood is being blighted by feeling judged and feeling guilty that they don't quite meet the mark. That they are not quite a good enough mum.

Are you one of them?

I am.

Aren't you exhausted by it all?

I am.

Don't you just want to step off the wheel of judgement and pressure and for once feel 100 per cent content in the knowledge that you are a bloody amazing mum and are doing a fantastic job?

I do.

I 've realised that to start to reclaim our right to enjoy motherhood we all need to be mentally fit for it – and this starts at home. It starts with us. It means ensuring that we as women are empowered to deal with whatever motherhood throws at us by being as prepared as possible – physically and mentally. It means every mum being prepared to embrace the magical and overwhelmingly joyous times of motherhood and being equally prepared to withstand and overcome the challenges too. Whatever form these challenges take, from the judgement we feel as mums, to the pressures of living up to the 'perfect parenting' images that bombard us and the mummy guilt those images create and mean we feel we do not quite meet the mark. To the strains and complex emotions and anxieties motherhood can instil in us. The changes our relationships go through and the lasting effects that becoming a mum can have on both our physical and mental well being.

I passionately believe that if we all stand strong against the pressures and judgement we are putting ourselves under; if we buck the trend and instead start to celebrate all our mummy wins, rather than concentrate on our perceived 'failures'; if we turn the 'Oh, no, we didn't leave the house all day today' to 'I've managed to keep my tiny human alive, fed and cuddled' – then our mum lives would be an easier place to reside. We would be armed to face the emotional pressure when we leave the front door, switch on the TV, open a magazine or read a Facebook status.

So how about we all make a promise? Not to the world or even to each other. But a promise to ourselves. How about every mum reading this right now (me included) promises herself that we will stop putting ourselves through all the judgmental crap and instead give ourselves a break? Ease off the pressure.

How about we promise to actually like ourselves more? To say, you know what, we are doing a bloody amazing job. I am proud of you.

How about instead of listening to the negative press we give ourselves, we instead shout from the rooftops:

I AM enough.

I AM worthy.

I AM doing a good job.

I AM a fantastic MUM.

Because you know what, my lovely friend?

YOU ARE!

xxxxx

AU REVOIR FOR NOW

Wow, my lovely, we made it. We have shared everything – and I mean everything, from my poo pants of shame through to seeing demons flying around my house and everything in between and thereafter. Thank you so much for sticking with me through it all and enduring some of the more cringeworthy of tales and the most toe-curling of honest confessions. You are bloody awesome and I think it's fair to say we are now mates for life.

I really hope you've enjoyed spending this time together, and I really hope too that if there was anything sucking your enjoyment of motherhood, reading this book has helped you (even in some small way) to start to reclaim it. Most importantly, I hope it's given you some honest insights, nonjudgmental support and a few good laughs along the way.

I hope more than anything that you are in a good place right now, and if you're not, that you know you're not alone, that there is a way to feel good again and back to being you.

As for me, well I am currently sitting at home during the summer holidays (no sniff of child care within a hundred-mile radius), putting the finishing touches to the book and trying not to puke with panic and fear that you are not going to enjoy it. All whilst my now four-and-a-half-year-old and three-year-old chase each other around the coffee table, dressed as Finding Dory and trying to give each other felt-tip pen tattoos (wish me luck!).

Tiny human tattoos aside, I'm happy and unbelievably relieved to tell you that I am in a strong place with my maternal mental health. I feel well and more mentally fit than ever before. Jamie, the girls and I are all doing great. We feel that we are at the start of a new chapter together, which has made us, for the first time in a long time, feel excited for what's to come next. Most importantly, we feel happy. Happy for the future, happy for our little family, and happy to be sharing it all together, just the four of us, no unwanted guests of the dark demon or depression variety in sight.

Day to day, I'm taking care of my two tiny humans and running my blog and Facebook groups, which are as busy as ever and filled with the most supportive and nonjudgmental mums I've ever had the pleasure to meet (if only virtually). The Every Mum Movement I launched earlier this year is going from strength to strength, gaining some high profile support and seeing me be all grown up and attending a variety of advisory discussion groups for the likes of NHS Health Education England, the Department of Health and visits to the Houses of Parliament. Where, believe it or not, I get to talk to influential people about my experiences of maternal mental health, all whilst dressed in heels(!) and clothes not covered in tiny human debris. (OK, you got me – less than the usual tiny human debris at least.)

I'm not ashamed to admit that whilst battling my mental illness and taking care of my tiny humans I lost myself along the way. I lost my confidence in myself and in what made me who I am. What made me Olivia. Not Olivia the wife or Olivia the mum but Olivia the person, with ideas, dreams and ambitions all of her very own, independent of family life. I have felt for a long time like a jigsaw puzzle with a few missing pieces and it's only since writing this book and starting The Every Mum Movement that I have started to feel like me again. Like a real life person, following her own path and her own ambitions.

The illness snatched away a lot of valuable things from me, which at the time I thought were lost forever. It stripped me of my self-belief and confidence. In a weird twist of fate, though, it also gifted me with a ferocious drive to 'do something'. It made me look at motherhood and parenting, and made me realise that there are so many areas of this experience that we feel too ashamed, too guilty or too silly to talk about. It made me decide to do something to change this so that other mums and mums to be are as well equipped as possible for this bonkers, wonderful and exhausting world of parenting. No judgement!

As a fellow woman and mum who has struggled with her mental health and experienced the judgement, pressures and guilt we can all feel as mums, I feel it is my duty to do all that I can to ensure other women have nonjudgmental support throughout their journey into motherhood and beyond. Not just in terms of being aware of their maternal mental health but in terms of ensuring every mum feels mentally fit to deal with the judgement and pressures to which we can find ourselves subjected. I want to let you and every mum out there know that you have me and a whole army of every mum allies in your corner all supporting you – no judgement!

Every mum deserves the right to enjoy motherhood. Let's do all we can to support one another to ensure that we all get to enjoy this right.

Love Liv xx

ACKNOWLEDGEMENTS

I have so many amazing people to thank for making this book a living breathing reality. I've been lucky enough to have two fantastic editors, therefore want to firstly say a HUGE thank you to my editor and friend Lucy Gilmour for believing in me and my writing from the very beginning and for turning my childhood dream of writing a book into a reality and to Rachel Kenny for listening to all my rambles and worries and offering fantastic advice and support along the way. A special thank you to my sister Natalie (and Ratfink) for being my fiercely honest and supportive additional editors of the book and for helping me breathe through the panic attacks of it finally getting published and to my amazing friends who have been on hand to read through bits of the book and brainstorm endless title ideas. (A special thank to Nicky, Vix and Emily for supporting my writing from the very start, to Sazza for your continued support and for letting me convince you to run 15K with me to raise awareness of PND despite never running before, and to Rebecca who would turn up on my doorstep and get me out of the house during some of my darkest days – I love you all!)

To my bro, Harry, and sis-in-law, Jenny, for your continued support and dedication to keeping me and Jamie well stocked in much needed vino fuelled party nights in our lounge when we couldn't find babysitters and for never thinking any of my ideas were ever too 'BONKERS'.

My battles with my maternal mental health stole a lot of precious things from me, however, they also gifted me with some incredibly special people too, therefore I would like to say a big thank you to my "mental health family" for being so wonderful, supportive and down right kick ass - you are all a true inspiration! (A special thank you to Emma Borg, founder of Acacia Family Support, Mental Health Campaigners Mark Williams, Eve Cavanan BEM, Lindsay Robinson, Nuala Murthy and Kate Dyson, founder of the Motherload – you have all been my much-needed rock at some point along this journey and I am proud to call you friends!) I would also like to thank the charity Mind for encouraging and supporting me to speak about my experiences of maternal mental health and to the wonderful Claire and Ellie in the Mind media team who, after years of talking on the phone and over email, I now get to call friends.

To my amazing mum, dad, Auntie Mary and Uncle Ernie for their unconditional support throughout my 39 years and for teaching me to believe that I can do anything I set my mind to (even write a book!), if I can provide the girls with even half of the wonderful things you've provided me with I will know I've done my job well.

I would also like to say an incredibly special thank you to all the incredible women (aka The No Bull Mums) who follow my blog and Facebook group. Words are simply not enough to thank you for the friendship, support and laughter you have given me over the last four years.

Finally, my last thanks go to my awesome husband and my beautiful, kind and headstrong little girls, thank you for everything, for believing in me, for always being there for me and for giving me the honour of being called your wife and your mummy. All three of you are my reason and I can't wait to see what the next chapter holds - "Love you in the whole wide world".

USEFUL RESOURCES

NATIONAL PREMATURE BIRTH AND CHILD BEREAVEMENT ORGANISATIONS

Bliss
www.bliss.org.uk

Tommy's
www.tommys.org

Child Bereavement UK
www.childbereavementuk.org

SANDS
www.sands.org.uk

NATIONAL MATERNAL MENTAL HEALTH ORGANISATIONS

After being diagnosed with PND I wish I'd had a check list of all the support organisations and websites I could have looked at, not only to find out more about the illness I was dealing with, but to also hear stories of other mums who were also going through or had been through what I was experiencing. The difference this would have made to my recovery and quality of life in general would have been immeasurable. Therefore, I've put together a list below of the organisations I've come across both in a personal and professional capacity over the last few years to help any mum reading this who currently needs some support or who would like to find out more about maternal mental health:

The Every Mum Movement
www.everymummovement.com

The Maternal Mental Health Alliance
www.maternalmentalhealthalliance.org

Mind
www.mind.org.uk

APNI (Association of Post-Natal Illness)
www.apni.org

APP (Action on Postpartum Psychosis)
www.app-network.org

The Birth Trauma Association
www.birthtraumaassociation.org.uk

The Samaritans
www.samaritans.org

Time to Change
www.time-to-change.org.uk

Online support and maternal mental health blogs

Below is a list of my top favourite blogs that talk honestly and openly when it comes to motherhood and mental health, including The Baby Blog I set up when battling through my experiences of Postnatal Depression and Postpartum Psychosis:

The Baby Bible
www.the-baby-bible.com

PND & ME
www.pndandme.co.uk

Smalltime Mum
www.smalltimemum1.wordpress.com

Have you Seen That Girl?
www.haveyouseenthatgirl.com

GLOSSARY

The following information has been taken from the Maternal Mental Health Alliance Website. For further information on all types of perinatal mental illnesses, their symptoms and treatment please visit: www.maternalmentalhealthalliance.org or www.nhs.uk

WHAT IS A PERINATAL MENTAL ILLNESS?

Perinatal mental health refers to a woman's mental health during pregnancy and the first year after birth. This includes mental illness existing before pregnancy, as well as illnesses that develop for the first time, or are greatly exacerbated in the perinatal period.

Examples of perinatal mental illness include antenatal depression, postnatal depression, anxiety, perinatal obsessive compulsive disorder, postpartum psychosis and post-traumatic stress disorder (PTSD). These illnesses can be mild, moderate or severe, requiring different kinds of care or treatment.

WHAT IS POSTNATAL DEPRESSION?

Postnatal Depression is a depressive illness which affects between 10 to 15 in every 100 women having a baby. The symptoms are similar to those in depression at other times. These include low mood and other symptoms lasting at least two weeks. Depending on the severity, you may struggle to look after yourself and your baby. You may find simple tasks difficult to manage.

Sometimes there is an obvious reason for PND, but not always. You may feel distressed, or guilty for feeling like this, as you expected to be happy about having a baby. However, PND can happen to anyone and it is not your fault.

WHAT IS POSTPARTUM PSYCHOSIS?

This is the most severe type of mental illness that happens after having a baby. It affects around 1 in 1000 women and starts within days or weeks of childbirth. It can develop in a few hours and can be life-threatening, so needs urgent treatment.

There are many symptoms that may occur. Your mood may be high or low and there are often rapid mood swings. Women often experience psychotic symptoms. They may believe things that are not true (delusions) or see or hear things that are not there (hallucinations).

This illness always needs medical help and support. You may have to go into hospital. Ideally, this should be to a specialist mother and baby unit where your baby can go with you. Although postpartum psychosis is a serious condition, the vast majority of women make a full recovery.

BONKERS

A Real Mum's Hilariously Honest Tales of
Motherhood, Mayhem and Mental Health

Olivia Siegl

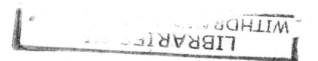

HQ

ONE PLACE. MANY STORIES

HQ
An imprint of HarperCollins*Publishers* Ltd
1 London Bridge Street
London SE1 9GF

This paperback edition 2018

1
First published in Great Britain by
HQ, an imprint of HarperCollins*Publishers* Ltd 2018

Printed and bound in Great Britain by
CPI Group (UK) Ltd, Croydon, CR0 4YY

MIX
Paper from
responsible sources
FSC™ C007454

This book is produced from independently certified FSC paper
to ensure responsible forest management.

For more information visit: www.harpercollins.co.uk/green